THE W

MARGARET THATCHER

SERIES EDITOR: BONNIE G. SMITH, RUTGERS UNIVERSITY

Published

ANWAR AL-SADAT: *Transforming the Middle East*
Robert L. Tignor

MUSTAFA KEMAL ATATÜRK: *Heir to an Empire*
Ryan Gingeras

MARGARET THATCHER: *Shaping the New Conservatism*
Meredith Veldman

QUEEN VICTORIA: *Gender and Empire*
Susan Kingsley Kent

Forthcoming

MALIK AMBAR: *Power and Slavery Across the Indian Ocean*
Omar H. Ali

SIMONE DE BEAUVOIR: *Creating a Feminine Existence*
Sandrine Sanos

LIN ZEXU: *Imperial China in a Globalizing World*
David Atwill

THE WORLD IN A LIFE

THE LIVES OF PEOPLE and the unfolding of earth-shaking events inspire us to love history. We live in a global age where big concepts such as "globalization" often tempt us to forget the "people" side of the past. The titles in *The World in a Life* series aim to revive these meaningful lives. Each one shows us what it felt like to live on a world historical stage and even to shape the world's destiny.

The lives of most individuals are full of activity and color and even passion and violence. The people examined in *The World in a Life* series often faced outsized challenges, but they usually met the great events of their day energetically. They lived amidst enormous change, as we often do. Their lives show us how to navigate change and to find solutions. They made fateful decisions, often with much soul-searching or—as often—on the spur of the moment and even intuitively. We have much to learn from these fateful past lives.

Their actions, however, were filled with complexity. Biographies in this series give a "nutshell" explanation of how important paradoxes and dilemmas have been in the stories of individuals operating on the world stage. Their lives become windows onto the complicated trends, events, and crises of their time, providing an entry point for a deeper understanding of a particular historical era. As such events and crises unfolded, these historical figures also faced crises in their personal lives. In the intertwined dramas of the personal and political, of the individual and the global, we come to understand the complexities of acting on the world stage and living in world history.

BONNIE G. SMITH
Rutgers University

THE WORLD IN A LIFE

MARGARET THATCHER

SHAPING THE NEW CONSERVATISM

MEREDITH VELDMAN

New York   Oxford
OXFORD UNIVERSITY PRESS

Oxford University Press is a department of the University of Oxford.
It furthers the University's objective of excellence in research,
scholarship, and education by publishing worldwide.

Oxford   New York
Auckland   Cape Town   Dar es Salaam   Hong Kong   Karachi
Kuala Lumpur   Madrid   Melbourne   Mexico City   Nairobi
New Delhi   Shanghai   Taipei   Toronto

With offices in
Argentina   Austria   Brazil   Chile   Czech Republic   France   Greece
Guatemala   Hungary   Italy   Japan   Poland   Portugal   Singapore
South Korea   Switzerland   Thailand   Turkey   Ukraine   Vietnam

For titles covered by Section 112 of the US Higher Education
Opportunity Act, please visit www.oup.com/us/he for the
latest information about pricing and alternate formats.

Published by Oxford University Press
198 Madison Avenue, New York, New York 10016
http://www.oup.com

Oxford is a registered trademark of Oxford University Press

Library of Congress Cataloging-in-Publication Data
Veldman, Meredith.
  Margaret Thatcher : shaping the new conservatism / Meredith Veldman,
Louisiana State University.
     pages cm. -- (The World in a Life)
  Includes index.
  ISBN 978-0-19-024897-0 (pbk., acid free : alk. paper) 1. Thatcher, Margaret.
2. Prime ministers--Great Britain--Biography. 3. Women prime ministers--
Great Britain--Biography. 4. Great Britain--Politics and government--1979-1997.
5. Conservatism--Great Britain--History--20th century. I. Title.
  DA591.T47V45 2015
  941.085'8092--dc23
  [B]
                                                           2015008402

Printing number: 9 8 7 6 5 4 3 2

Printed in the United States of America
on acid-free paper

FOR GRAHAM

CONTENTS

LIST OF ILLUSTRATIONS

LIST OF MAPS

ACKNOWLEDGMENTS

I AM VERY PLEASED to have the chance to thank *The World in a Life* series editor Bonnie Smith for giving me the chance to write this book, as well as Priscilla McGeehon and Charles Cavaliere for editorial support. The endnotes and bibliography indicate my many debts to numerous scholars of contemporary Britain, but I must particularly acknowledge John Campbell, whose masterful biography of Thatcher made this book possible; Dennis Kavanagh, whose work in the late 1980s first shaped my views of Thatcher and Thatcherism; and the Margaret Thatcher Foundation, which has made its remarkable and invaluable website www .margaretthatcher.org free and available to all. The late Bill Heyck read the entire manuscript and provided much-needed encouragement. George Esenwein of the University of Florida, Guy Ortolano of New York University, Amy Whipple of Xavier University, and Kirk Willis of the University of Georgia reviewed the manuscript for Westview Press and helped make this a better book. Randy Nichols came up with the shape of the first chapter, proofread the manuscript, and endured countless Thatcher-centered conversations. Jeremy Nichols offered a student's reading and helped me see that I was finished. Thank you all for your careful reading and thoughtful comments. Finally, I dedicate this book to Graham Nichols, whose passion for the Now pulls me out of the Past—and I appreciate it.

ABOUT THE AUTHOR

MEREDITH VELDMAN received her bachelor's degree in history from Calvin College (Grand Rapids, Michigan) and her PhD in modern European history from Northwestern University (Evanston, Illinois). She is an associate professor at Louisiana State University, where she teaches courses in modern Britain, modern Ireland, and twentieth-century Europe. An award-winning teacher, Veldman helped design and served as the rector of Louisiana State University's Global Connections Residential College. She is the author of *Fantasy, the Bomb, and the Greening of Britain: Romantic Protest, 1945–1980* and co-author of *The West: Encounters and Transformations* and *The Peoples of the British Isles: A New History from 1688 to the Present.*

INTRODUCTION

THE SECOND DAUGHTER of a provincial grocer, Margaret Roberts Thatcher was not born to privilege or power. She was not an original thinker; few of her teachers regarded her as particularly clever. She had little interest in literature, music, or art and no interest in popular culture in any form. What she did possess, however, was a remarkable physical constitution (she needed little sleep and was never ill), a phenomenal capacity for hard work, and a resolute ideological certainty alloyed with political adaptability and a populist sensibility. The results changed British society and helped reshape the political culture of the Western world.

As one of the central founders of New Conservatism, Thatcher fought to shatter the post–World War II political consensus, the mainstream agreement that the central state must regulate national economic and social life to ensure full employment and the citizen's welfare from cradle to grave. Thatcher came of age when the postwar consensus was at its strongest. By the time she walked onto the world stage as leader of Britain's Conservative Party in 1975, however, the ideals of social citizenship forged in the tumult of World War II had begun to break down under the pressure of economic crisis. The resulting political confusion gave Thatcher the chance she needed. As prime minister of Britain from 1979 to 1990, she initiated the move of vast areas of the economy from public or state control to private ownership. More generally, Thatcherism both fed and fed upon a growing skepticism about state activism and governmental power—although, paradoxically, under Thatcher's guidance the power of Britain's central state grew, in some areas enormously.

Any understanding of the history and assessment of the impact of the New Conservatism demands examination of Thatcher's biography and influence, but such an examination also allows us to explore the central themes and tensions of postwar British and, more broadly, Western political history. Thatcher grew up in a world in which the British Empire was a given; by the 1970s, most of that empire had disappeared. As prime minister, Thatcher oversaw Britain's retreat from one of its last imperial outposts: Hong Kong, which reverted to Chinese control in 1997 after 156 years as a British territory. But Thatcher also led her nation into war to repel Argentina's invasion of the Falkland Islands, a relic of the empire with no strategic or economic value. The loss of empire and, more broadly, the shifting global power relations that explain imperial disintegration, provided the context for Thatcher's ardent nationalism and much of her political appeal.

Fittingly enough, Thatcher first ran for office in 1950, the year that Britain followed the United States into war in Korea (the first "hot" conflict of the cold war), and she first became a government minister in 1961, the year that Britain submitted its initial, unsuccessful application to join the European Economic Community (the forerunner of today's European Union). Here we see highlighted two options for Britain's postimperial identity—as an Atlantic power in "special relationship" with the United States or as part of "Europe." For Thatcher, the choice was always very clear. The cold war not only confirmed Thatcher's tendency to see both domestic and international political affairs in terms of "us versus them," it also solidified her perception of Britain's alliance with the United States as the central defining feature of "us." In turn, this Atlantic orientation accentuated Britain's ambivalent relationship with its European partners—a continuing theme in the politics of postwar Europe.

Yet Thatcher's historical significance extends beyond the realm of politics. As the first female leader of a major Western political party and the first (and so far only) woman to be Britain's prime minister, Thatcher might be assumed to be a feminist icon. She is not. Despite her own personal choices—to pursue a demanding political career while her children were still very young and her husband often away on his own business pursuits—Thatcher skillfully appropriated and utilized conventional gender ideology in her rise to power. Recognizing the strength of popular anxiety about the widening role of women, and the way in which this anxiety reflected wider concerns about postwar social and cultural transformation, Mrs. Thatcher promised a return to traditional solidities. Her career thus offers us an illuminating glimpse into changes and continuities in the contemporary history of Western gender roles and relations.

Perhaps the best reason to study the life, career, and impact of Margaret Thatcher, however, is because it is such a good story. Few modern politicians inspired such levels of admiration and revulsion. When Thatcher died in 2013, political leaders around the world hailed her as a champion of individual freedom and the economic savior of Britain. At the same time, "Thatcher death parties" erupted in many British cities. Many of the celebrants at these parties had not even been alive when she was in office; they recognized, however, that Thatcher had played a crucial role in shaping their world.

CHAPTER 1

THE SOCIAL DEMOCRATIC CONSENSUS

IN THE CRUCIAL MONTHS OF 1942 and 1943, as Allied forces from El Alamein to Stalingrad, from Midway to Palermo, began to push the German and Japanese armies back, a teenaged English girl sat with her father in their sitting room and listened to the radio reports of the war's progress. The wall in front of them held a large world map; on it they used pushpins to keep track of the Allied advances. An enormous admirer of Prime Minister Winston Churchill, Margaret Roberts never doubted that Britain would win World War II, or what became known in Britain as the People's War. She was, however, shocked by the People's Peace that followed. Three decades after the war ended, when Margaret Roberts—now Mrs. Thatcher—became Leader of Britain's Conservative Party, she pushed her party and then her country into repudiating that peace. Mrs. Thatcher's election in 1979 marked a turning point in British and in western European history, and it marked the advent of New Conservatism as a global political force.

In the spring of 1940, Nazi Germany's forces swept across northern and down through western Europe. Astounded by the scale and speed of the German advance, journalists coined a new word: *blitzkrieg*, lightning warfare. By the end of May, exhausted and demoralized French and British troops clustered on the small beachhead of Dunkirk on the English Channel as the German Luftwaffe pounded them from above. With the loss of their entire army a genuine possibility, the British hastily improvised an evacuation. Over 200,000 British and 140,000 French soldiers made it to the safety of British shores, most carried in navy ships, but a small number rescued by civilians who volunteered their fishing boats and pleasure craft and risked their lives to bring their lads home.

Immediately, the Dunkirk evacuation became one of the founding *myths*—not falsehoods, not fairy tales, but the stories through which people make sense of themselves and by which they forge a national identity—of the People's War. Dunkirk signaled that World War II would be fought and won not just by professional soldiers but by ordinary civilians working all-out to

DUNKIRK LITTLE SHIPS. *The role of the "little ships"—private shipping and pleasure boats—in the Dunkirk evacuation became a key element in the public memory of the People's War.*

provide the food and fuel to run the machinery of total war. A few months after Dunkirk, the war entered a new phase and the People's War took on new meaning. Over the summer of 1940, the Luftwaffe and the Royal Air Force (RAF) engaged in the high-stakes Battle of Britain, the struggle for control of the skies above the English Channel (and thus, for the Germans, a necessar victory if they were to mount an invasion of the British Isles). The RAF won the Battle of Britain and no German invasion occurred. Instead, the Blitz began. For ten months, German bombers pummeled British cities, night after horrifying night; during these months, it was safer to be a British soldier than to be a British civilian. The deaths of 30,000 men, women, and children, and the destruction of 3 million homes demonstrated the reality of the People's War.

Out of the People's War came the People's Peace, the conviction that the sufferings of the war could only be redeemed if postwar society looked dramatically different from its prewar predecessor, if a new and more just social order resulted. This conviction was not confined to Britain. Across war-torn Europe, groups and individuals spanning the political spectrum demanded that the long fight against Nazism be made worthwhile, that Europeans work not to reconstruct the politically divided and economically depressed societies of the prewar era but rather to build anew. Scarred by the experience of mass unemployment in the 1930s, they pointed to the combatant governments' success in mobilizing their economies for total war. If governments could regulate economies for warfare, why could they not regulate economies for welfare—why could they not use the massive power of the central state to allow citizens to fare well?

In Britain, these questions were asked, and answered, remarkably early in the war. At the beginning of 1942, long before an Allied victory even looked likely, Churchill appointed a governmental committee to explore the issue of postwar reconstruction. Chaired by William Beveridge, a social reformer and head of the London School of Economics, this committee quickly concluded that prewar British society must not be reconstructed as it was; rather, it must be redesigned. The committee's recommendations, published as the Beveridge Report in December 1942, proved to be one of the most influential documents in the history of twentieth century Europe. In almost fairy-tale language, Beveridge identified five "giant evils" that threatened the British public: Want, Disease, Ignorance, Squalor, and Idleness (or, in less poetic terms, poverty, lack of health care, lack of education, inadequate housing, and unemployment). To slay these giants, the Report recommended three weapons: (1) an activist government economic program to ensure full employment; (2) an array of welfare services ranging from old-age pensions to family allowances; and (3) comprehensive health care, free at the point of provision. A radically expanded definition of citizenship—often called social citizenship—drove these recommendations. To be a citizen, the Beveridge Report assumed, was not only to have legal and political rights, not only to expect the state (the national government) to provide protection from foreign invasion or criminal attack, but also to expect, *to have the right to*, a decent standard of living, adequate educational opportunities, comprehensive health care, and security in times of sickness, unemployment, or old age—and to count on the state to promote and defend those rights.

State action to blunt the sharp edges of capitalism was not new to Britain or to Europe in the 1940s. As far back as the 1870s, the Conservative German chancellor Otto von Bismarck had pioneered the state provision of unemployment and health insurance for limited sectors of the population. In Britain, it was also a Conservative prime minister, Benjamin Disraeli, who in the 1870s introduced the first significant social welfare legislation in the areas of housing and public health. In both the pre–World War I and the interwar years, democratic governments throughout western Europe expanded various social welfare measures as they struggled to incorporate the growing urban industrial classes into the national community and compete in the international

THE BEVERIDGE REPORT. *This cartoon from the popular* Daily Mail *newspaper illustrates the widespread public excitement about the Beveridge Report and its plans for a new Britain. The soldier holds up a mug bearing William Beveridge's profile and the words "Social Security." Behind him, World War II rages on—a fight, the British people had decided, to defeat not only dictators abroad but also social injustice at home.*

economic and military arenas. In many ways, then, the Beveridge Report simply built the welfare state on foundations already constructed over the preceding decades. Pre–World War II welfare provisions, however, added up to what has been called the ambulance state—the idea of the state swooping in to save the poorest in dire emergency. In contrast, in the welfare state envisioned by the Beveridge Report, services available to every member of society would provide security from cradle to grave. Everyone paid into the fund that assisted parents of young children, the sick, the disabled, the elderly, and the unemployed; and at various stages of their lives, everyone benefited.

Unlike most government reports, the Beveridge Report became a bestseller, with over 600,000 copies bought by 1943. Two copies were even found in Hitler's Berlin bunker after the war. The Beveridge Report not only outlined what would become the postwar British welfare state; it also became the model for social welfare programs across Europe and thus is one of the founding documents of European *social democracy*. In a social democracy, the elected government accepts the responsibility of ensuring a decent standard of living for its citizens. To achieve this goal, the government assumes two functions. First, it oversees the welfare state: the citizen's guarantee of security in life's exigencies. In western Europe, the postwar welfare state included not only old-age pensions (what Americans call Social Security) and unemployment, sickness, and disability benefits, as in the United States, but also family allowances (usually a per-child payment to assist parents in the demands of raising a family), comprehensive health care, and free higher education for all who qualified. By the end of the 1950s, the average western European working-class family received only 63 percent of its income from wages, with the substantial remaining income drawn from welfare benefits.

To provide a decent standard of living for all, the social democratic state also assumes a second function: management of the economy to ensure full employment. Social democracy is not socialism. Social democratic governments sought not to eliminate but rather to regulate private enterprise and free market competition so as to avoid the mass unemployment of the pre–World War II period. Many western European states, therefore, nationalized (or removed from private ownership) economic concerns that had featured high rates of joblessness in the interwar period—for example, coal and shipbuilding—or those sectors that are vital for the public good, such as transport and utilities. Most businesses, however, remained in private hands.

In addition to nationalization, postwar social democracies turned to Keynesian economics to fulfill their promises of full employment. Named after its principal theorist, the English economist John Maynard Keynes, Keynesian economics is essentially a shorthand for the fiscal and monetary policies that postwar governments used to steer their economies toward steady economic growth without either the trauma of high inflation rates (usually linked to an economy growing too fast) or the tragedy of mass unemployment (the hallmark of economic depression). Keynes believed firmly in capitalism, but he saw the free market as, by its very nature, unstable and not therefore guaranteed to create full employment. The job of governments, then, was to manage demand through spending and taxation to ensure job creation. To help governments do this, Keynes devised many of what are now commonplace economic policymaking tools, including standardized national income accounting (the concept of the gross national product, or GNP) and the multiplier (the idea that if the state employs a worker, that worker will spend money, which will in turn create more jobs—and thus the initial public investment is multiplied).

Labor relations formed the final piece in the social democratic project. The western European societies that emerged from World War II were still recognizably the products of the Industrial Revolution. Still largely fueled by coal, these societies made things—steel, machine tools, ships, cars, domestic appliances, textiles, toys. Manufacturing drove the engines of their economies and thus the industrial worker who serviced that engine stood in a paramount position. Recognizing the crucial role that wage rates and worker productivity played in determining national prosperity, governments in postwar social democracies worked with not only the management boards of nationalized industries but also private employers and trade unions to broker employment contracts. Called *corporatism*, this policy gave unions unprecedented political and economic influence in the decades after World War II.

Across western Europe, policymakers and ordinary people agreed on the social democratic shape of their postwar societies. No matter what the specific political complexion of their state— alternating between two- and three-party coalitions (as in Denmark and the Netherlands), dominated by leftist Social Democrats (Sweden) or rightist Christian Democrats (West Germany and Italy), or in constant political flux (France)—western Europeans regarded state regulation of the economy to ensure full employment as not only economically necessary but morally right, and agreed that the expansion of social welfare programs was both a prerequisite and a guarantor of democracy. Most western states devoted about 15 percent of government spending in the 1950s to social welfare programs, such as child allowances, health insurance, housing subsidies, and old-age pensions. All regulated the market economy through Keynesian measures and most adopted some version of nationalization or state control of key industries. By the early 1960s, government-controlled industries accounted for about 40 to 50 percent of employment in many western European states.

There was, of course, no single European social democratic model. For example, most western European states provided universal health care for their citizens through a mix of private and public insurance programs, rather than following the British choice of a national health service. Other welfare provisions also varied. The French provided equal access to pensions and disability insurance for both men and women and established networks of child day-care and after-school programs to enable working women to have children, while the British and West German models encouraged married women to stay home by granting them fewer benefits. Management of the economy also differed. Scarred by the experience of the Great Depression, the British government nationalized much of heavy industry on the assumption that public control would better assure full employment but, in contrast to the French, rejected the idea of a planned economy. The postwar West German government associated both state control of industry and national planning with Nazism and so opted for a social market approach that emphasized corporatist management and negotiation.

Despite these differences, throughout western Europe, the postwar years saw the social democratic revamping of economies and societies as governments, private industry, trade unions, and citizens' groups all worked together to develop the networks that would widen access to education, guarantee adequate housing and health care, and provide economic security through full employment and welfare provision in all of life's phases and emergencies. By the mid-1950s, the benefits of the social democratic project were widespread across European populations. Western European children—the recipients of free vitamins, vaccinations, and school lunches—became the healthiest in the world. The French came to call the postwar era *Les Trente Glorieuses*—the thirty glorious years. West Germans talked about the *Wirtschaftswunder*—the economic miracle. In British history, the post–World War II years are known as the Age of Affluence, a time of full employment and rising real wages, unprecedented educational opportunity, and mass consumerism.

In the 1970s, however, the Age of Affluence ended. Margaret Thatcher became prime minister in 1979, after a decade of economic stagnation had ravaged first the British and then most western economies. Her three terms in that office marked a decisive break with the social democratic consensus and a turning point in British and global history. Declaring herself to be a politician of conviction rather than consensus, Thatcher worked to dismantle many of the features of the social democratic state and to remake British political culture. Her influence, moreover, extended far beyond Britain. The Thatcherist model of social, economic, and fiscal policymaking helped shape a New Conservatism that reoriented economies and societies across the world.

The 1970s saw the social democratic consensus cracking as governments struggled to cope with unprecedented economic crisis. Yet economics alone does not explain Thatcherism or the New Conservatism. In Thatcher's view, the social democratic political consensus that had emerged from the war was not only economically and fiscally unsustainable but morally wrong. Her experience of the People's War led her to very different conclusions about what British society was and in what direction it should head. Thatcher opposed the nationalization of key industries as an unwarranted expansion of the state into the free market; she believed that the welfare state encouraged irresponsible and even immoral behavior, and more generally, she regarded government taxation and government spending as necessary evils, to be kept within sharp limits. An outsider by class, region, and above all gender, she never shared in the consensus and, once she took power, she helped shatter its hold on British political life.

Thatcher's political views drew heavily on the ideology of *classical liberalism.* A tricky word, *liberalism* means something rather different in the United States today than it does in Europe—**and this book uses the word in its European sense.** In the United States, liberalism has come to be associated with Big Government, an activist state that uses its power of taxation to redistribute wealth from the rich to the less well-off (as well as with social views that challenge traditional moral codes covering sexual behavior and gender roles). In Europe, however, liberalism has retained its original meaning as an ideology of individual freedom. In its classical and its European definition, liberalism views the individual, rather than class, nation, race, or hierarchical privilege as the basic building block of society, and argues that the state's role is to remove obstructions to individual freedom. Drawing on the Enlightenment theories of the British political economist Adam Smith, liberals exalted free market competition as the "invisible hand" that ensures economic prosperity for both the individual and society. Embraced in the nineteenth century by Europe's emerging middle classes, liberalism challenged both aristocratic paternalism and socialist egalitarianism, and instead espoused the values of meritocracy, in which the most talented and highly educated would rise to the top of the social, economic, and political pyramid through their own hard work. Liberals thus championed the free market and advocated sharp limits on the state's power to intervene in economic and social life. This liberal emphasis on minimizing the economic role of the state was often summed up in the French phrase *laissez-faire*, roughly translated "let it be" or "leave it alone."

The roots of Thatcher's New Conservatism in liberal economic theory explain why she and other New Conservatives are often also labeled as neo-liberals (much to the confusion of generations of students). New Conservatives like Thatcher saw liberal economics as a way to meet the challenges of the late twentieth and twenty-first centuries. They argued that only markets, not states, were fast and flexible enough to respond to rapid technological change and to the transition from economies built on heavy industrial production to those based on the dissemination of information and services. Whether they were correct remains hugely controversial. There can be little controversy, however, about the impact of New Conservatism. During the 1980s and 1990s, enormous sectors of many western economies moved from public into private hands, and the regulations restraining those private hands dwindled. The postwar commitment to maintaining full employment disappeared, replaced by the conviction that inflation, not joblessness, poses the greatest threat to capitalist prosperity and democratic stability. As the ideals of social citizenship eroded, new political cultures based on lowered expectations came into being.

In all of this, Thatcher played a crucial role, yet she encountered defeat as well as victory. State spending did not decrease during her years in office and while she spoke often about how important it is that individuals and communities decide their own affairs, in Britain her reforms vastly increased the power of the central state at the expense of local governments and civic agencies. She sought to revive Britain as a global power, but her politics left it a far more divided nation. Her legacy remains hotly contested. She was, and she remains, one of the most controversial political leaders to play a role on the twentieth-century world stage.

| IN THE MIDDLE, YET ON THE |
EDGE: 1925–1947

HOW CAN A PERSON BE in the middle, yet on the edge? This paradoxical position was the central theme of Margaret Hilda Roberts Thatcher's childhood and adolescence. Margaret grew up in the middle of England and in the middle of the British class system. But in interwar Britain, living in the middle meant growing up on the periphery of political power and cultural influence. Margaret's core values and assumptions resulted from her upbringing outside the ranks of the politically influential— and her determination to break into those ranks as soon as possible.

The convictions that guided Mrs. Thatcher as prime minister and that shaped her contribution to the making of the New Conservatism took shape during her childhood when she lived above her father's grocery store in the town of Grantham. Region, class, and family worked together to shape Margaret Roberts and to create what would later be known as Thatcherism.

When Margaret was born in 1925, regional identities were still very powerful in British society. It mattered that Margaret grew up in the East Midlands, a region in the middle of England.

MAP 1. THE UNITED KINGDOM

It mattered because it meant Margaret grew up outside "the South," the locus of political power and cultural influence in twentieth-century Britain. The key to the South's dominance is, of course, London. The cultural and political ascendancy of London in British culture is absolute; one has to imagine Washington, D.C., somehow merged with New York City and Los Angeles to come up with an American parallel. Growing up in Grantham, then, Margaret grew up on the outside. Described by one of its town clerks as "a narrow town, built on a narrow street and inhabited by narrow people," Grantham was provincial, both in the geographic sense of being in the provinces, outside the environs of the

capital city, and in the cultural sense of being limited, unsophisti-
cated, adrift outside the main currents of intellectual, cultural,
and political life.[1]

Even more than region, class mattered in interwar Britain, and
it mattered that Margaret grew up in a lower middle-class family,
outside the circles of the established political elite. By the 1920s,
the Conservative Party had expanded from its original constituency of the hereditary aristocracy and country gentry to embrace
big businessmen and financiers. Linked by a common upbringing
involving attendance at a public school (not, as in the United
States, a state school that is free and open to all, but rather an expensive, single-sex boarding school open to a select few), followed
by three years at Oxford or Cambridge University, this new upper
class emphatically did not include people like the Roberts family.
All her life, Margaret struggled against the prejudices and privi-
leges of an elite that regarded her grocer's origins with disdain.

It also mattered that Margaret did not grow up in "the North."
A concept as much as a region, the North embraced the heavy
industrial heartland of England. Much like Scotland and Wales,
the North possessed a very distinctive regional identity shaped
by the Industrial Revolution of the eighteenth and nineteenth
centuries and the emergence of a proud working-class culture.
This culture in many ways defined itself against the liberal ideology of the dominant middle class: collectivist rather than individualist and convinced that self-help ideology was yet another
lie foisted on workers by bosses eager to maintain the status quo.
Out of this northern working-class culture came the trade union
movement that, in partnership with middle-class socialists, built
the left-wing Labour Party. Trade unionism and the Labour
Party's evolutionary (rather than revolutionary) brand of socialism expressed the collectivist and anticapitalist values of northern
working-class culture, a culture to which Margaret never belonged and against which she defined herself throughout her political career. In addition, the trade union movement served as an
important route to political participation and power for ambitious

young activists. This route was as closed to young Margaret as was access to a public school education.

The strong sense of working-class identity and the collectivist values that shaped the union movement and Labour Party politics were antithetical to a small businessman like Margaret's father, Alfred Roberts. Instead, Alfred embraced a stern individualism and a belief in taking care of one's own family and making one's own way in life, as he had done. Alfred left school at age thirteen for full-time work. In 1913, when he was twenty-one years old, he moved to Grantham to work as a shop assistant. World War I broke out a year later. Alfred tried to enlist several times, but his poor eyesight ensured that he was never accepted. Unlike many men of his age, then, Alfred was able to move rapidly ahead with his life plans, even during the war years. In 1917, he married Beatrice Stephenson, a twenty-eight-year-old seamstress. Two years later, Alfred and Beatrice bought their first grocery store, located on a busy street at the edge of a working-class neighborhood that supplied most of his customers. (Wealthier shoppers patronized the posh shop located downtown.) More like a general store than an American supermarket, the Roberts' small corner shop served not only as a purveyor of foodstuffs and cigarettes but also as a local post office and hence as the distribution center for old-age pensions (in American terms, Social Security payments). Alfred and Beatrice both worked in the shop (and in the second grocery store that they purchased some years later), even after Beatrice gave birth to Muriel in 1921 and to Margaret four years later.

The Roberts' family life thus revolved around the grocery store. From early on, both girls worked in the shop with their parents. Although official opening hours were Monday through Saturday from 8:00 a.m. until 7:00 p.m., the fact that the family lived right upstairs meant that customers never hesitated to ask them to open up before or after hours. Margaret grew up in a world of buying and selling, of counting change and balancing accounts, of paying bills and collecting debts. She never abandoned her belief that a national

THE CORNER SHOP. *Living above and working in the family's grocery store inculcated Margaret Roberts Thatcher with her father's work ethic and liberal economic philosophy.*

economy was simply an expanded version of the corner grocery store, and that the free movement of trade undergirded individual and national prosperity. As Thatcher put it in her memoirs, "There is no better course for understanding free market economics than life in a corner shop."[2]

Significantly, Alfred's chief rival in the grocery store business was not the posh downtown store where the town's wealthier residents shopped but rather the nearby local co-op. Cooperatively owned grocery stores, run not for an owner's profit but for the benefit of the customer members, began in the nineteenth century as part of a multifaceted cooperative movement that sought to soften the edges of industrial capitalism. Linked to the Labour Party, the co-op represented the collectivist, communally oriented, working-class identity that Alfred rejected completely. As a small business owner and a self-made man, Alfred identified himself with the middle class and firmly embraced middle-class liberal economic and social values.

The grocery stores earned the Roberts family a comfortable but by no means lavish living. Their upstairs flat did include a bath and toilet but no hot water and certainly none of what the British called "mod cons"—modern conveniences such as a washing machine or refrigerator. Beatrice made all the family clothes, a fact that Thatcher later recalled with some regret: "My mother was a very good dressmaker but my sister and I often felt that our things were different from others."[3] Beatrice and Alfred had scrimped and saved to buy their grocery store, and for them, frugality was not just a means to an end, but an end in and of itself, a moral virtue and a way of life.

When the Roberts did have free time, they spent it in church. On a typical Sunday, Margaret and her family attended Sunday school at 10:00 a.m., and church service at 11:00; after Sunday dinner came a second Sunday school session and then the 6:00 evening service. Alfred was a lay preacher (although not an ordained minister, he preached at local churches on Sundays) and Beatrice's only social activities were the church sewing circle on Tuesdays and the church ladies' guild on Fridays. The teenaged Margaret became an active member of the church youth group.

Margaret's parents were staunch Wesleyan Methodists. The Wesleyan part is important. During the nineteenth century, British Methodism fragmented into a number of independent denominational groups, each with a strong class base. Some Methodist groups espoused a marked egalitarianism, preached a message of social justice, attracted working-class members, and became important bases for the Labour movement. In contrast, Wesleyan Methodism attracted the middle strata of British society—men and women like Alfred and Beatrice—with a message that emphasized individual achievement over social concerns and that equated Christianity with the rigorous practice of a practical moral code and a strong emphasis on hard work. According to Thatcher, "We were taught what was right and what was wrong in considerable detail. There were certain things you just didn't do and that was that. Duty was very, very strongly engrained into us."[4]

Methodism was important in shaping Margaret in another, less overt way. In England, there is no separation of Church and State. The Anglican Church is the Church of England: Anglican bishops sit in parliament, the head of state (the monarch) is also the head of the Church, and the public schools, the training grounds for the political elite, require their pupils to attend Anglican chapel services. Although England is a far more secular society than the United States, even today the Church of England retains a great deal of political and social influence. In the interwar era when Margaret came of age, Anglican preeminence was pronounced in every area of English society—but Margaret was a Methodist. Thus religion, like region and class, placed her outside the circles of privilege and power in interwar Britain.

It did not, however, place the Roberts family outside the circles of privilege and power in interwar Grantham. Alfred's sense of duty extended to local activism as well. He was president of the Rotary Club, chairman of the Local Savings movement, on the board of governors of Grantham's grammar school, and, throughout the 1930s and 1940s, a town councilman (an elected office) and then an alderman (appointed by the council). Alfred first ran for office in 1927 to ensure that the local Labour Party did not win a majority on the council. As a businessman, Alfred was convinced that Labour government would mean higher taxes, a prospect that he loathed. Throughout his many years in office, Alfred developed a reputation for his financial skill and his concern with keeping the rates (local property taxes) low. The fact that much of local government spending benefited people who were too poor to pay property taxes violated Alfred's sense of right and wrong. As he explained in a speech in 1937, "the people who don't pay the rates are sponging on those who do."[5] Throughout the years of World War II and after, Alfred served as alderman and even, in 1945–1946, as mayor (a largely honorary position), but in 1950,

THE ROBERTS FAMILY. *In 1945, Alfred Roberts became mayor of Grantham and the Roberts family posed for a rare family portrait.*

Labour won a majority on the town council. A year later, the council replaced Alfred with a local Labour supporter. He resented his dismissal for the rest of his life, as did his daughter.

Alfred was a dutiful rather than a doting father. The Roberts household radiated with ambition, not affection; frugality, not fun, was the order of the day. As Thatcher put it, "Life wasn't to enjoy yourself; life was to work and do things."[6] When she became a national political figure in the 1970s, Thatcher spoke often of her close relationship with her father. There is, however, little evidence of such closeness; these recollections resulted either from a calculated political choice, an effort to frame an appealing personal biography, or perhaps simply from wishful thinking. The adult Margaret rarely visited her father after she left home nor did he visit her; her own children did not know their grandfather, even though they lived only a few hours away. Yet the lack of a close personal relationship does not negate the enormous influence that Margaret's father had on her life. As an adolescent, Margaret often accompanied her father to campaign appearances and local political meetings. More important, Alfred bequeathed to Margaret her political ambitions and convictions, as well as his strong sense of duty and his belief in an absolute, clearly delineated moral code.

Like many ambitious girls of her generation, Margaret adopted her father rather than her mother as a role model. Beatrice taught Margaret how to sew, cook, keep house, and manage a budget. She seems to have been an austere, parsimonious woman who enjoyed saying no. One of her mother's favorite words, Thatcher recalled, was "serviceable": utility always trumped beauty or fun. The young Margaret, however, "longed for the time when I could buy things that were not serviceable."[7] Beatrice did not share in the political discussions between father and daughter, and offered her daughter little affection or attention. Thatcher admitted, "After I was fifteen, we had nothing more to say to each other. It wasn't her fault. She was weighed down by the home, always being in the home."[8] It seems likely that Margaret's extreme competitiveness and ambition stemmed in part from a desire to win from the world the praise that she never received from her mother.

Her determination to win showed up an early age. In 1935, ten-year-old Margaret won a scholarship to the Kesteven and Grantham Girls' School. In the two-track interwar English state school system, a scholarship to grammar school was the only avenue to a university education open to working-class and lower middle-class students. Had Margaret failed the scholarship examination, she would have been shunted onto the nonacademic line, to leave school at age fourteen for full-time employment. Grammar school gave Margaret the chance to move out of the lower middle class, and out of Grantham, and she made the most of it. When she arrived at the school, she did not strike her teachers as a particularly bright or creative girl. Determined to prove them wrong, Margaret worked hard at her studies and year after year came out at the top of her class through sheer diligence and hard work. But at grammar school, as in much of her life, the theme of "the outsider" colored Margaret's experience. Alfred and Beatrice would not let their daughter attend school dances or parties. Talking to an interviewer in 1980, Thatcher recalled that her schoolmates "would do far more of those things—out with other people where there was laughter and fun."[9] With her social world strictly limited to the local Methodist church, Margaret stood apart from most of her classmates.

Margaret's childhood coincided with a tumultuous time in British economic life. By the time she was born in 1925, the devastating impact of World War I on the British economy had become clear. Britain experienced a national depression in 1921, the effects of which kept economic production at a low ebb throughout most of the decade. The worldwide Great Depression that struck in 1929 shattered any recovery that had begun. The British economy remained depressed until the outbreak of World War II, with unemployment never dropping below 10 percent between 1923 and 1939. This long-term depression, however, did not afflict all British regions and industries in the same way. The North was hit especially hard. The heavy export industries that had propelled Britain forward in the world's first Industrial Revolution now found their markets gone and their technology out of date. Some coalmining areas saw unemployment rise above 50 percent; in the shipbuilding town of Jarrow, 80 percent of the working population was without a job. In the Midlands and South, however, the unemployment figures were far lower as workers found employment in new industries—such as small electric consumer goods, rayon and other synthetics, and automobiles—geared toward the home market. Thus, in Britain the interwar years were both the Locust Years, a time of hardship and hunger, and a period that saw increased consumer and leisure spending, the spread of vacation time, and the transformation of the automobile from rich man's toy to middle-class family necessity. It all depended on where one lived and what one did for a living.

Living in the Midlands, working in the grocer's shop, Margaret and her family were spared the full fury of the economic storm that ravaged northern industrial cities and mining villages. Grantham's factories did not shut down and as Margaret later noted, "Our family business was also secure: people always have to eat, and our shops were well run." She did recall that every day walking to school she passed "a long queue waiting at the Labour Exchange, seeking work or claiming the dole [unemployment benefit]" but "none of our closest friends was unemployed."[10] Once again, then, Margaret's place in the middle was crucial. Her very moderate experience of the Great Depression meant that she, unlike many Britons growing up hungry and desperate in the North, saw no reason to question the viability of free-market capitalism or to wonder if the state should play a larger role in mitigating the ravages of poverty and systemic unemployment.

As Margaret made her way through grammar school, a deepening crisis engulfed Europe. With the Great Depression still squeezing the global economy, the Nazi regime in Germany began a program of military rearmament and territorial expansion. Since the early 1920s, British governments—Liberal, Labour, and Conservative—had sought to rectify what they perceived as the wrongs inflicted on Germany by the Versailles Treaty after World War I. This policy of appeasement took on a new intensity after Adolf Hitler, head of the Nazi Party, became chancellor in 1933 and then, within six short months, dictator of Germany. British policymakers believed that through negotiations and the correction of legitimate grievances, they could tame Hitler. This assumption explains why British policymakers did not respond forcefully to such aggressive violations of the Versailles Treaty as Hitler's resumption of the military draft in 1935, the remilitarization of the Rhineland in 1936, and the annexation of Austria into a Greater Germany in March of 1938.

By the summer of 1938, however, war looked likely after Hitler demanded that Germany annex the Sudetenland, the territory in Czechoslovakia that was home to a large percentage of Czechoslovakia's German minority population. Under pressure from the British and French governments, the Czechs made a number of concessions to Hitler but refused to agree to outright annexation. As gas masks were issued to every British man, woman, and child in preparation for the widely expected chemical warfare, Neville Chamberlain, the Conservative Prime Minister, flew to Munich to engage Hitler face to face. The resulting Munich Agreement forced the Czechs to cede the Sudetenland to Germany; it also, Chamberlain insisted, "saved Czechoslovakia from destruction and Europe from Armageddon."[11]

The Munich Agreement is now seen as a fundamental failure to confront the real threat posed by Hitler to European peace. Thatcher would later remember her father as a strong opponent of appeasement and of the Munich Agreement. Her father did not, however, oppose Munich at the time, nor did most British men and women. In September of 1938, the vast majority of the British public—including Alderman Roberts—cheered the Agreement and praised the British prime minister, Neville Chamberlain, for averting a world war. Church bells rang across the country in thanksgiving and jubilation as Chamberlain returned from Munich and announced that he had achieved "peace in our time."[12] This peace, of course, lasted for only a few months. The following spring German forces invaded the rest of Czechoslovakia and then in September marched into Poland. The British and French governments declared war on Germany on September 3, 1939. World War II had begun.

Gender, nationality, and age shaped Margaret's war. Unlike many of the men who would later be her colleagues or rivals in government, she was not dropped far from home and thrust into the company of strangers from other classes and regions. She did not know the camaraderie of soldiers welded into a single unit by the struggle for survival, nor did she confront the horrors—far exceeding anything endured by the British—that continental populations suffered under Nazi rule. Too old to join the

40 percent of British infants and schoolchildren who were evacuated (usually without their mothers) from cities and placed in the homes of strangers, Margaret was also too young to be drafted for war work. She did not undergo the rigors of overtime in a munitions plant or of farm labor as a Land Girl.

Margaret's war did not, then, confront her with new and life-altering experiences. It did not force her to reevaluate her assumptions and ideals or to question the basic social order. Instead, her war confirmed what she already firmly believed: that Great Britain was a force for good in the world and that state power had the inexorable tendency to encroach on individual freedom and responsibility.

Margaret fought her war on the home front. The British *home front* was just that, a front in a wide-ranging total war that demanded the mobilization of civilians as well as soldiers. In the summer of 1940, the Royal Air Force won the Battle of Britain: it prevented the German *Luftwaffe* from establishing control of the skies above the English Channel and the British Isles, and so blocked a German invasion of Britain. But victory in the Battle of Britain led not to peace but to the horrors of the Blitz, the large-scale bombing of British cities. Through the autumn and winter of 1940 and 1941, when the Blitz was at its most intense, more British civilians died from enemy action than did soldiers. Attacks on cities continued throughout the war, and by the conflict's end, over 67,000 British civilians had been killed.

The bombs began to fall on Grantham when Margaret Roberts was just one month shy of her fourteenth birthday. A major engineering center with three steel factories and a munitions plant on its outskirts, Margaret's hometown made an appealing target for German bombers. Over the next few years, the Luftwaffe hit Grantham 21 times, killed approximately 70 people, and injured another 200. Alfred Roberts helped organize Grantham's defenses against air raids and often served on air raid duty in the evenings. With no backyard in which to dig an air raid shelter, the Roberts family sat under the kitchen table during the more than 380 bombing alerts. They knew, however, that they were safer than Margaret's older sister, Muriel, who had moved to Birmingham in 1938 to train as a physical therapist. One of England's most important and heavily populated manufacturing centers, Birmingham came behind only London and Liverpool in the numbers of bombs dropped upon it.

In between bombs came the cold, dark, slog to victory. The wartime National Government, an all-party emergency administration headed by the Conservative leader Winston Churchill, assumed control of most aspects of the economy by the end of 1940. Over the next five years, the National Government presided over an immense expansion of state intervention in and regulation of economic and social affairs. Government directives told people where to work, what to eat, and how to dress. From the length of women's skirts to how much water to run in the bathtub to the application of lipstick—the state's hand seemed omnipresent. One Canadian diplomat noted, "Living in London is like being an inmate of a reformatory school. Everywhere you turn you run into some regulation designed for your protection."[13] As the numbers of rules and directives piled up, so too did taxes: by the war's end, the standard rate of income tax stood at 50 percent, with the top rate at 97.5 percent. Most citizens recognized the expansion of state power as essential in a time of total war. But the fact remains that during her most formative adolescent years, Margaret experienced the state as an all-powerful, intrusive, frequently overweening force. It was not a government that did too little, as many Britons experienced during the Great Depression, but rather a government that seemed to want or need to do everything.

For most people, rationing constituted their most direct encounter with state control. To reduce imports (borne on ships vulnerable to German submarine attack) and to ensure the fair distribution of goods (and thus maintain civilian morale), the government established a comprehensive system of rationing. Gasoline was strictly rationed until 1942, and then withdrawn from the market entirely. Food rationing, first introduced in

January 1940 for red meat, butter, and sugar, was gradually extended to tea, eggs, margarine, jam, and canned foods. Fish, chicken, and fresh fruit and vegetables were "off ration"—but were often simply unavailable, while imports such as banana and lemons disappeared completely. Working with her parents behind the counter of the grocery store, Margaret occupied the front lines of the domestic fight to reduce consumption and to stretch resources. Grocers like Alfred in many ways became government agents, forced to master an ever-expanding and always changing set of rules and rationing standards—and to explain those rules to, and to enforce those standards upon, their exhausted, irritable, and frightened customers.

Rationing extended beyond food. Weary housewives were frequently frustrated in their quest for essential household goods, such as frying pans, toothbrushes, batteries, and dishes. "Make do and mend" became the order of the day. For Alfred and Beatrice Roberts, however, "make do and mend" had long been a guiding principle; the Roberts family ethos of duty and useful action served the home front well. The wartime hardships of the British home front thus did not alter but rather affirmed the Roberts' way of life: the war was difficult but not a sharp break from what had gone before. Alfred continued to pursue his career in local politics. Margaret occasionally joined Beatrice in serving tea at the soldiers' canteen, but she remained focused on her personal ambitions, studying Latin, becoming Head Girl at Grantham Grammar, and then leaving home for university.

In October of 1943, Margaret was notified that she had a place at Somerville College, one of Oxford University's all-women colleges. The nearby University of Nottingham had accepted Margaret for undergraduate admission, but she never considered attending there. In 1943, and still to a large degree today, Oxford and Cambridge—"Oxbridge"—shaped Britain's political class. In the years between1950 and 1964, for example, 80 percent of Conservative Party parliamentary candidates who had attended any university had attended Oxbridge. For a politically ambitious, provincial young woman from the lower middle class, Oxford or Cambridge offered the only real route out— out of the confines of Grantham, out of the Midlands, southward, toward power.

Oxford made Margaret Roberts Thatcher's political career possible, yet it did not transform her in the way that the university years often change young men and women: by challenging their long-held beliefs and values. Margaret used her Oxford years to acquire information and organizational skills rather than to explore new ideas or to expand her worldview. At Oxford, Margaret remained very much the outsider. Her regional background, her class, her religion, her gender, and her politics all placed her outside the prevailing currents. But rather than diving in and letting the current sweep her along, Margaret swam against the stream. The experience bruised her; it left her with a lifelong hostility toward the sort of people who dominated Oxford—university academics and privileged elites—and it heightened her aggressive determination to come out on top.

Rationing, shortages, and, of course, the drafting of most young men for military service meant that for the first two years of her university life, Margaret's Oxford was a strange, shrunken place, with a limited roster of social events. Nevertheless, it remained a place of privilege and power, quite daunting to an eighteen-year-old girl with a provincial accent who had hardly ever traveled outside her hometown. The university still drew most of its students from the ranks of the upper and upper-middle classes, who came to Oxford via the well-worn but exclusive public school path. As a grammar school girl and the first in her family to go to university, Margaret admitted that she "felt shy and ill at ease in this quite new environment." Her autobiography, written fifty years later, still betrays her sense of resentment at not being part of the class that slid naturally into Oxford life: "I might have had a more glittering Oxford career, but I had little money to spare."[14]

Margaret studied chemistry. In the all-female environments of her grammar school and college, science was not demarcated as male; Somerville College, in fact, possessed a stellar reputation for its scientific prowess. In addition, chemistry was in many ways an obvious choice for an individual who liked precision and believed that "good" and "useful" were interchangeable terms. Margaret showed little real enthusiasm for the subject, but she knew she would have to support herself when her university career ended. By the 1930s, chemistry-based research in the production of products such as synthetic rubber, chemical pesticides, synthetic fibers, and food additives showed itself to be a profitable area for economic development. As Beatrice might have said, chemistry was "serviceable," and Margaret never expressed much interest in literature or the arts. With her eyes on the future, she worked hard in her studies and did well, although most of her professors regarded her as competent and diligent rather than intellectually distinguished.

But Margaret never intended an academic career: her real passion lay not in chemistry but in politics. From the moment she arrived in Oxford, she threw herself into Conservative student politics and by the time she left Oxford, she knew that she wanted to become a Conservative Member of Parliament (MP). Aspiring politicians across the political spectrum had long used Oxford—which has educated twenty-five of Britain's prime ministers—as a jumping-off point for a national political career. It was in the world of Oxford *politics* rather than in the lecture hall or laboratory that Margaret for the first time confronted the problem of being a woman in a very male world. It was as if a huge "Men Only" sign hung over the university's two key political launch pads. The first, the Oxford Union, bills itself as the "world's oldest debating society." The Union served (and to an astonishing degree continues to serve) as "the playground where generations of aspiring politicians strutted, trying out on one another the *mots* and mannerisms they would later take to Westminster [Parliament]."[15] Women, however, were banned from participating in Union debates in the 1940s—just as they could not join the second key political organization, the Canning Club, an exclusive debating club for Conservatives at Oxford. Once again, Margaret stood on the outside, looking in.

But, faithful to a pattern she would repeat throughout much of her life, she built her own "inside" instead. She joined the only political organization open to her—the Oxford University Conservative Association (OUCA)—and marshaled her formidable organizational skills to accentuate its presence in Oxford through a packed program of parties, debates, and speakers' series. At Margaret's events, "you could always be certain that the food and drink would last out, and you could also be certain that you would probably meet somebody you had never met before."[16] Crucially for her later career, Margaret arranged for Conservative Party politicians of national standing to speak at OUCA events and so began developing important contacts and establishing a place for herself within the party. Yet even at the OUCA, Margaret was known more for her organizational skills and diligence than for her ideas or her speeches. Most of her peers recalled that she spoke very little—a sure sign of how out of place she felt in the university milieu.

While Margaret remained unusually quiet at university events, she had no trouble speaking when she was in a more familiar setting. Throughout her university years, she relied on the Wesley Society (the Methodist student organization) and local Methodist churches for religious solace and a ready-made social circle. Margaret's choice to remain Methodist within Oxford University, a bastion of the Established Church of England, reinforced the already substantial barricades that stood between her and typical Oxford undergraduate life. Particularly in her first two years, Methodist activities consumed much of her spare time. Like her father, she now became a lay preacher, traveling on Sundays from village to village around Oxford and delivering sermons in small Methodist churches. Standing in the pulpit Sunday after Sunday, Margaret gained invaluable experience in public speaking and the art of persuasion. It meant she had regular contact with British men and women who, like her, were not part of the Anglican upper classes that dominated the university—and who would later form much of her political base.

In the middle of 1945, as Margaret was climbing her way up the officer ranks of the OUCA, the war ended. On the surface, the advent of peace brought little real change for Margaret: she continued to pursue her degree, her involvement in the OUCA, her lay preaching. Peacetime did mean the return of men to Oxford and so a rapid expansion in her heretofore largely Methodist-oriented social life. Margaret drank her first sherry, smoked her first cigarette, and danced at her first ball.

Far more important to her, however, was the disbanding of Churchill's all-party coalition government that had governed Britain since 1940 and the decision to resume normal party political competition. In July 1945—just two months after Germany's surrender and while the war in Japan was still raging—British voters went to the polls for the first general election since 1935. Margaret threw herself into the campaign. Although she was only nineteen years old, she served as warm-up speaker for the Conservative Party candidate running to be Grantham's MP. The newspaper report of her stump speech shows that she focused on the need to vote Conservative to ensure Churchill's continuing leadership in the postwar world. Tracing the progress of British armies around the world with pins on a wall map, Margaret had never doubted that British pluck and Churchill's leadership would win World War II: "I had the patriotic conviction that, given great leadership of the sort I heard from Winston Churchill in the radio broadcasts to which we listened, there was almost nothing that the British people could not do."[17]

Margaret assumed, as did many members of the British public and certainly Churchill himself, that the Conservatives were bound to win a majority of seats and form the first postwar government. When the results were announced, Margaret was, then, "shocked and upset." Labour had won a colossal victory and Clement Attlee was now prime minister. "I simply could not understand how the electorate could do this to Churchill," Thatcher later recalled.[18] The election results of 1945, however, were not a repudiation of Churchill's wartime leadership. Margaret's admiration for Churchill was not unusual: he had proven an inspiring war leader, and his position as one of the Big Three (with the Soviet leader Josef Stalin and the American president Franklin D. Roosevelt) seemed to affirm what most Britons saw as their country's incontrovertible global might. But in casting their ballots that July, British voters were looking ahead to peacetime rather than back to the war, to domestic matters rather than to foreign policy, to the reconstruction of postwar British society—and on these issues, Churchill and his young admirer were out of step with the majority.

In hindsight, Labour's victory should have surprised no one. Despite Churchill's personal popularity, his Conservative Party was tainted by its association with both appeasement and the economic hardships of the 1930s. Even more important, during the war years, British public opinion tilted distinctly to the left. As the bombs rained down and the numbers of the dead mounted, British men and women became determined to win not only the war but also the peace. They demanded a new social order. Convinced that the economic depression and social inequalities of the 1930s explained the appeal of dictators like Mussolini and Hitler, they argued that the survival of political democracy depended on economic democracy. Impressed by the capacity of the state to mobilize the economy for warfare, growing numbers of British men and women began to ask why the state could not intervene in peacetime to ensure welfare. They came to believe that citizens had the right to fare well, to a minimum standard of living, established and defended by state action.

The Labour Party recognized this cultural shift. When party political competition resumed in Britain in the summer of 1945, Labour fully endorsed the recommendations of the Beveridge Report in calling for a universal and comprehensive welfare state. Labour candidates campaigned with slogans such as "Fair Shares for All." Churchill and the Conservatives, however, expressed less enthusiasm for the Report or the promise of radical social change that lay behind it. The electorate made its choice clear. Labour won with 393 seats to the Conservatives' 210 (with 12 seats going to the Liberal Party). Such a majority gave the new Labour government a mandate for pressing ahead with the Beveridge recommendations and with constructing a social democratic state in Britain.

In her memoirs, Thatcher described the social democratic turn embodied by the results of the election of 1945 as "a collective loss of common sense." In her view, most Britons had wrongly concluded that "the 'lesson' of wartime was that the state must take the foremost position in our national life and summon up a spirit of collective endeavor in peace as in war." But, she continued, "The 'lessons' I drew were quite different." She explained that the war taught her "that the kind of life that the people of Grantham had lived before the war was a decent and wholesome one, and its values were shaped by the community rather than by the government."[19] The war confirmed what was, rather than illumined what could be. As an admirer of Churchill and his government, Margaret did not dispute the need for wartime regulation or intervention, but she saw such governmental expansion as a necessary evil, to be curtailed as soon as possible.

The idea of a universal and comprehensive welfare state, moreover, contradicted the individualist ideology of self-help so firmly instilled in Margaret by her parents. In the Roberts' view, making benefits available to all, regardless of need or effort, would only foster a culture of irresponsibility and immorality. Margaret would not have disagreed with the reaction of one shop assistant to the Beveridge Report, who described the promise embodied in social democracy this way: "It is like marrying a rich husband without having to have a husband."[20] Margaret, however, believed firmly that one should always have to have the husband.

Margaret's firm Conservative partisanship and enthusiastic Conservative activism further set her apart from most of the university community during her time at Oxford. Dame Janet Vaughan, who was on the faculty at Somerville and became its principal in 1945, said of Margaret: "She was an oddity. Why? She was a Conservative." Vaughan admitted that although she used to invite many students to her home at the weekends, she never invited Margaret: "She had nothing to contribute, you see." Similarly, one of Margaret's fellow undergraduates at Somerville confessed, "We used to laugh at Margaret Roberts when she knocked on our doors and tried to sell us tickets for the Conservative Club ball."[21] Conservatism in general, and her brand of Conservatism in particular, seemed outmoded, a relic of the past to be swept away by the social democratic current. Margaret, however, saw the postwar social democratic consensus as a kind of socialist virus: "What I learned in Grantham ensured that abstract criticisms I would hear of capitalism came up against the reality of my own experience: I was thus inoculated against the conventional economic wisdom of post-war Britain."[22]

CHAPTER 3

MRS. THATCHER GOES TO PARLIAMENT: 1947–1970

IN THE 1950s, MARGARET ROBERTS became Margaret Thatcher. She moved from Oxford to Essex, from single life to marriage and motherhood, from a single rented room to a very comfortable suburban home, from a restricted income to substantial wealth. She also fulfilled her longtime ambition to enter national politics, becoming a Member of Parliament in 1959. Her personal transformation paralleled wider social and political change as western European societies moved from rationing and restrictions to the unprecedented consumerism and widening economic opportunities of the Age of Affluence. A dominant thread in the fabric of affluence, however, was a renewed focus on domestic life and on the woman's role as wife, mother, and homemaker. Thatcher's prioritizing of her political career over her preschool children stood out as exceptional in a society that defined a mother's proper place as the home rather than the House of Commons, but in a skillful deployment of rhetoric against reality, she presented herself as an embodiment rather than as a deviation from the dominant female domestic ideal. The gender anxieties of the 1950s and 1960s became a weapon Thatcher wielded with great skill as she pressed ahead in political life.

These years of prosperity and domesticity were also years of political consensus. Throughout western Europe, the dominant political parties and their voters shared a fundamental commitment to social democracy and to the ideal of social citizenship that served as its basis. Thatcher did not share this consensus, but as a pragmatic and an ambitious politician, she moderated her opposition and tended to toe the Conservative Party line, which in these years followed a social democratic course. By the end of the 1960s, however, increasing social and economic tensions, coupled with a growing backlash against what became known as permissiveness, signaled that the political consensus was beginning to crack and that the constituency for a New Conservatism was emerging.

In 1947, Margaret Roberts left Oxford University with a B.Sc. degree in chemistry—a solid achievement but one she had already deemed fundamentally useless for propelling herself into politics. She had to make a living, however, and so she went to work as a laboratory researcher at a firm called BX Plastics, where she earned a significantly lower salary than men in the same position. Typical of Margaret, she impressed her supervisors with her work ethic. Her fellow researchers were less impressed: "Snobby Roberts" and "Aunty Margaret" dressed too formally and took herself too seriously. For Margaret, however, politics, not plastics, was already her real job. BX Plastics provided her with a necessary income while she fought to get a footing on the political ladder. She devoted most of her spare time to the local Young Conservative Association, where she made no secret of her political interests or ambitions.

Her big break came just a year after she had left Oxford. In 1948, Margaret attended the Conservative Party Conference as a representative of the Young Conservatives. At the conference an acquaintance introduced her to the chairman of the Dartford Conservative Association—an introduction that, as her biographer John Campbell notes, "changed her life."[1] A large town in the county of Kent, Dartford voted solidly Labour. Dartford Conservatives could not hope to win, but with the right candidate, they

CANDIDATE MARGARET ROBERTS CANVASSING IN DARTFORD IN 1951. *Although a single working woman with high political aspirations, the young candidate made sure to present herself as a model of "house-wifely" common sense.*

could pare down Labour's majority and inject some excitement into the local Conservative culture. Labour's dramatic victory in 1945 had shocked Conservatives across the country. Desperate to avoid being labeled out-of-touch and out-of-date, they scrambled for ways to associate themselves with youth and vigor. To the disgruntlement of some of Dartford's more traditionally inclined Conservative rank and file, but to the delight of the national media, the Dartford Conservative Association selected a 23-year-old single woman as the party candidate.

For the next three years, Dartford voters encountered the incredible force of Margaret's ambition as she campaigned for a parliamentary seat in two general elections (1950 and 1951). She lost both times, but winning was never an option and not really the point. The Dartford candidacy provided Margaret with the opportunity to prove herself as a campaigner and as a Conservative. In these tasks, she succeeded. Membership in the local Conservative Party rose by 37 percent, an increase widely attributed to the young candidate's assiduous politicking. Moreover, in her campaigns, Margaret first showed one of her strongest political assets: her ability to make traditional gender ideology work for rather than against her. Later in her career, Thatcher grew impatient with the idea that she was a "woman candidate" rather than simply a candidate, but she always recognized and capitalized on the attention that her femaleness attracted. Intrigued by the novel sight of a young woman running for national office, reporters from the national press packed her campaign meetings, where she impressed them with her enthusiasm and her attention to detail. Always dressed impeccably, Margaret made the most of her youth and her good looks, and was careful to present herself not as a feminist or a career woman, but rather as a practical, domestically inclined young lady. Speaking out against high taxation rates, for example, the youthful candidate insisted, "The Government should do what any good housewife would do if money was short—look at their accounts and see what was wrong."[2]

The Dartford campaigns propelled Margaret onto the national stage and even attracted international publicity. The excitement her campaigns generated explains why, in 1952, a national weekly magazine asked her to contribute an article to a special edition celebrating Queen Elizabeth's coronation and the advent of the so-called New Elizabethan era. Entitled "Wake Up, Women!" Margaret's article insisted that women could and should combine demanding careers with marriage and motherhood. She called for more women in politics and asserted, "The idea that the family suffers is, I believe, quite mistaken." Although only two women had ever served in a British Cabinet up to that point, Margaret dared to ask, "Why not a woman Chancellor—or a woman Foreign Secretary?"[3]

Margaret's insistence on a woman's ability to combine marriage and a career was more than theoretical: in 1952, when she wrote "Wake Up, Women!" she was no longer Margaret Roberts but Mrs. Denis Thatcher. The wedding took place not in Grantham but in London, with a reception in Kent hosted not by the father of the bride, but by one of Margaret's Conservative Party supporters. The arrangements emphasized Margaret's break with Grantham and her family—and probably also indicate some parental displeasure with her choice of husband. A wealthy businessman, Denis Thatcher was several years older than Margaret and divorced. The couple wed in a Methodist chapel but afterward joined the Church of England. They attended church only occasionally; religious observance, always so central to Margaret Roberts, ceased to matter much to Margaret Thatcher. From this point on, Mrs. Thatcher saw little of her parents and rarely returned to Grantham. Now the wife of a millionaire, she embraced a lifestyle of conspicuous consumption that contrasted sharply with her parents' devotion to frugality and serviceability.

Margaret Thatcher's personal shift from scarcity to abundance mirrored that of the wider culture. The later 1940s were years of extreme hardship throughout Europe. In occupied Germany, rations barely reached starvation levels in the mid-1940s, while in much of eastern Europe, living standards were catapulted back to the 1700s. Compared to such suffering, the British were comfortable, but many British men and women, nonetheless, found it hard to believe they had won the war. Britain had spent all it had and more to wage total war; it entered the postwar era in deep financial crisis. The United States demanded immediate repayment of wartime loans, while ongoing military commitments in places like Greece, Palestine, and Malaya drained British resources. In desperate need to boost national income through the sale of exports, the Labour Government embarked on an austerity program. Continuing the wartime direction and regulation of the economy, it diverted labor and materials into the export market while restricting domestic consumption through even more extensive rationing than during the war. In 1946, for example, bread went on ration for the first time, and in 1947, potatoes. That year the Labour government also cut the butter and meat rations and imposed sharp restrictions on the use and availability of electricity. Soap, clothes, gasoline, and coal (the main source of domestic heating) also remained strictly rationed.

Economic recovery was just beginning when President Harry Truman's administration in the United States made the crucial decision to pour nearly $13 billion in aid into the European economy through a program called the Marshall Plan. Britain received $3.2 billion, more than any other recipient. The combination of Marshall funds and the Labour austerity program proved effective: between 1946 and 1950, British exports rose by 77 percent, and Britain, as well as the rest of western Europe, embarked on the Age of Affluence, two decades of unprecedented economic expansion and mass prosperity. On the average, western European economies grew by almost 4 percent a year during the 1950s and 1960, with some, such as the Italian, growing even faster. Britain's growth rates were less dramatic, averaging 2.8 percent in these years, but even at these lower rates, ordinary people experienced a dramatic leap forward in living standards. As the weekly earnings of the average Briton rose by an astounding 130 percent in the decade after 1955, spending on household items like vacuum cleaners and refrigerators jumped 115 percent and car ownership rates skyrocketed.[4]

In Britain, the transformation from austerity to affluence coincided with a shift from Labour to Conservative rule. The Conservative Party won the general election of 1951 and remained in office until 1964. Thatcher herself recalled the Conservative victory in 1951 as "the reawakening of normal happy life after the trials of wartime and the petty indignities of austerity."[5] Economic growth and mass prosperity assured that the 1950s were a decade of Conservative dominance.

Yet for Thatcher these were years of political frustration. In the long run, Thatcher's marriage made her political career possible. She always downplayed the advantages she gained from Denis's money, but she admitted "that with no private income of my own there was no way I could have afforded to be an MP on the salary then available."[6] In the short run, however, Thatcher's marriage made her political career decidedly more difficult, even though she quit her work as a chemist and focused on her political ambitions. She and Denis made their home in London and she began "reading for the Bar"—the process of clerking and studying to qualify as a barrister. Thatcher had little interest in the law in and of itself, but the socially prestigious and highly paid position of barrister seemed a good steppingstone into politics. She expected to be quickly rewarded for her work in Dartford with a "safe seat," a candidacy in a solidly Conservative constituency that would guarantee her election to the Commons. Instead, she was turned down again and again by candidate selection committees, whose members could not, would not, endorse a married woman as their candidate.

The reluctance of these committees to choose a young married woman as a candidate for Parliament reflected a wider cultural shift, the postwar return to domesticity. In the wake of the gender upheaval caused by total war, men and women in western European and American societies retreated to what they perceived as normalcy, the belief that the woman's role should be centered on the home and family. As an article in a popular British woman's magazine explained to its readers in 1961, "Ask any man if he'd rather his wife worked or stayed at home and see what he says; he would rather she stayed at home and looked after his children, and was waiting for him with a decent meal and a sympathetic ear when he got home from work. . . . You can't have deep and safe happiness in marriage and the exciting independence of a career as well."[7] Paradoxically, the number of married women in paid work grew during the 1950s, the result of the voracious employment needs of expanding economies and of the new emphasis on consumerism. By 1961, 50 percent of all working women in Britain were married. This work, however, was usually low-wage and often part-time, overwhelmingly seen as ancillary to the woman's *real* job of homemaking. Thatcher's desire to combine a demanding political career with marriage thus aroused skepticism within local Conservative Party branches.

This skepticism grew more pronounced after August 1953 when she gave birth to twins, Mark and Carol. Although in these years the percentage of married women employed outside the home was rising, most women stopped working after the birth of their first child and did not resume paid employment until their last child reached school age. Thatcher, however, finished her final set of bar exams just four months after the twins' birth, began work in a firm specializing in tax law in January 1954, and continued her quest for a safe parliamentary seat—a very unusual and unpopular set of decisions within the context of the 1950s. The local committees of Conservatives who were charged with selecting the party's parliamentary candidates could not believe that the mother of twin toddlers could be serious about a political career. An observer (and Thatcher supporter) at one such meeting reported that when committee members expressed their concern about her ability to juggle both motherhood and a career, Thatcher's reply about her "excellent nanny . . . did not a lot of good."[8] Despite the fact that Thatcher received the enthusiastic backing of the Conservative Party's Central Office, selection committee after selection committee turned her down.

Finally, however, Thatcher's long wait paid off. In 1958, the Conservative constituency of Finchley, a solidly Conservative north London suburb, selected her as its candidate. When a general election was called the next year, Thatcher's parliamentary victory was ensured. (She would hold the Finchley seat for thirty-two years.) Her election won national attention: women constituted fewer than 3 percent of the MPs that year, and Thatcher was the only one with young children at home. The *Finchley Press* reported that she had "attracted vast national publicity as a woman who was 'going places', appeared on TV, was heard on the radio, filled columns in the national press."[9] But the *London Evening News*' headline—"Mark's Mummy Is an MP Now"— typified the coverage: Thatcher was newsworthy not because of her policies or politics but because of her gender. Her male colleagues tended to ignore or patronize her; one recalled, "She appeared rather over-bright and shiny . . . We all smiled benignly as we looked into those blue eyes and at the tilt of that golden head."[10] Thatcher recalled the "male chauvinist hilarity" that greeted her every day in the corridors and meeting rooms.[11] As an attractive woman with young children, however, she also received opportunities afforded to no other novice MP, including a commission to write a series of articles on the challenges faced by working mothers for a London daily newspaper, which described her as "Britain's most talked-about, hard-hitting new woman MP."[12] She was invited to be on the television program *Any Questions* and asked by the *Evening News* (London) to write a series of articles on the challenges faced by working mothers.

Within the wide space provided by all of this publicity, Thatcher utilized rather than rejected the domestic ideal; she fashioned a public image that allowed her to epitomize domesticity and wield it as a political weapon. Always dressed impeccably, she made the most of her youth and her good looks; even more important, she was careful to present herself not as a feminist or a career woman, but rather as practical and domestically inclined. One of her tactics in Dartford, for example, had been to hold meetings in Conservative Clubs—male bastions that barred women from entering, unless they were barmaids. Skillfully turning a ban into a blessing, Margaret registered herself as a barmaid, entered the clubs, and in an early demonstration of the efficacy of the photo op, posed for photographs pulling pints for her male supporters. A young woman serving drinks to older men—an image not of threat but of consolation, even titillation and desire.

Thatcher used domesticity to articulate her liberal politics by adopting the persona of the practical housewife, skilled in

WASHING UP, OCTOBER 1974. *Although a Cabinet member and soon to be Leader of the Conservative Party, Thatcher always made sure to emphasize her homemaking skills. October 1974.*

keeping domestic accounts, who must call spendthrift politicians to task. According to a newspaper report of her very first speech as a parliamentary candidate in 1949, "Miss Roberts stressed that the security a family could have by saving its own money, buying its own house and investing, was far better" than the security gained through public housing schemes.[13] Five months later she told a meeting of Conservative women—most of them certainly older than her—"Don't be scared of the high-flown language of economists and cabinet ministers, but think of politics at our own household level."[14] The "our" is crucial, even though at this point she was a young single woman who spent her days in a laboratory, her evenings on political platforms, and her nights in a rented room. Yet by metaphorically donning the housewife's apron, the young Margaret Roberts here claimed the moral authority of the domestic ideal—as Mrs. Thatcher would throughout her political career.

At the same time, Thatcher used liberal individualism to reconcile the domestic ideal with her own political career. During the decade of her climb into Parliament, Thatcher openly challenged critics who doubted her ability to combine politics and family life. Her "Wake Up, Women!" article in 1952 insisted that women belonged in the political sphere. She expanded on this theme two years later in a piece she wrote for a Young Conservatives publication. Now a mother as well as a wife, Thatcher moved beyond the rather passive argument of "the family does not suffer" to a more active assertion: that a woman's work enhances family life. Dismissing outright the idea that "a woman's place is in the home," she argued, "it is essential both for her own satisfaction, and for the happiness of her family that [a woman] should use all her talents to the full."[15] This gendered formulation of the liberal doctrine that the fulfillment of individual desires works for the communal good became Thatcher's mantra as she moved ahead in political life. In an unusually forthright interview after her election in 1959, she continued to assert that she cared for her family but made it clear that her career served her own needs: "I should vegetate if I were left at the kitchen sink all day. I don't think the family suffers at all through my political ambitions." Long before the phrase "quality time" was coined, Thatcher was a fierce advocate of it, asserting that with careful organization and "a first-class nanny-housekeeper to look after things in the wife's absence," a woman could combine motherhood with a demanding career.[16] She did not seem to be aware that few families could afford the "first-class nanny-housekeeper," although she did acknowledge that Denis's money made her political career possible.

As was typical of a British upper-class mother, Thatcher spent little time with her children. In 1957, the Thatchers purchased a large, eight-bedroom house in Kent, a long commute from central London where Thatcher worked from early in the morning until the early evening—and once she was an MP, through many nights spent at Parliament. (Until 1999, the House of Commons met from 2:30 p.m. until late in the evening when it was in session.) In her autobiography, Thatcher noted that she "always telephoned from the House [of Commons] shortly before six each evening to see that all was well"—a rather revealing admission of how little contact she had with her children, even before they were sent away to boarding school (Mark at age eight, Carol at age nine).[17] In her daughter's assessment, "my mother's political ambitions—and the single-mindedness with which she pursued them—eclipsed our family and social life." But, she noted, "No woman gets to the top by going on family picnics and cooking roast beef and Yorkshire pudding for Sunday lunch with friends."[18] Certainly no male prime minister was called to account, as was Thatcher, for the amount of time he devoted to his career at the expense of his family.

Thatcher's rise to the top began in 1961 when she joined the Conservative government in a junior position at the Ministry of Pensions and National Insurance. Thatcher's background in tax law qualified her for this position, but even more important was her sex. Prime Minister Harold Macmillan had three women in his government and so when one of them resigned, he looked for another woman to take her place. Thatcher became only the second woman with children to serve as a government minister—and the first to do so while her children were young (the twins were eight years old at the time). Her superior John Boyd-Carpenter admitted that he thought that Macmillan's appointment of Thatcher "was just a little bit of a gimmick on his part. Here was a good-looking woman and he was obviously . . . trying to brighten up the image of his government."[19] Boyd-Carpenter revised his early judgment; Thatcher impressed him with her willingness to put in long hours and her phenomenal attention to detail. As he put it, "Despite the fact that to the male eye she always looked as though she had spent the morning with the coiffeur and the afternoon with the couturier, she worked long and productive hours in the Ministry."[20]

Thatcher remained in Pensions until 1964, when Labour took office again after a closely won general election. The Conservatives lost control of the government but Thatcher continued her climb upward. In the British parliamentary system, a party that is no longer in office appoints a "shadow government," a group of opposition spokespersons who "shadow" or parallel the actual government ministers. Thatcher served as the shadow junior minister in pensions, housing, and economic policy. In October 1967, a woman in the Shadow Cabinet stepped down; Thatcher then moved up to serve as member of the Shadow Cabinet for power, transport, and education. She was "the Conservative Opposition's maid of all work."[21] No other Conservative politician was shifted around so much—and again, gender helps explain why. In Thatcher's own words, "I was principally there as the 'statutory woman' whose main task was to explain what 'women' . . . were likely to think."[22] She was not popular—seen as too talkative, too bossy, and too opinionated by male colleagues unaccustomed to dealing with women as political or professional equals—but she solidified her reputation for reliability and productivity. No one, however, anticipated that she would soon become leader of the party and then of the country. This dismissive description of her by a *Sunday Telegraph* reporter in 1969 was fairly typical: "Mrs Thatcher is a very pretty woman in a soft suburban way with a nice mouth and nice teeth and large round dolly eyes, like a candy box tied off with two shiny bows of blue ribbon." In the same article, Thatcher herself insisted that "no woman in my time will be Prime Minister."[23]

In making her way up through the ranks of the Conservative Party in the 1960s, Thatcher had to battle against not only the prevailing cultural ideology of female domesticity but also the prevailing political ideology of social democracy. By the time Thatcher became an MP, the radical plans of the postwar Labour government had become the political status quo. The shift from Labour to Conservative government in 1951 did not herald any effort to dismantle the welfare state. In its election manifesto of 1949, the Conservative Party even claimed the welfare state as its own achievement: "The Conservative party has welcomed the new social services which it has done so much to create. We regard them as mainly our own handiwork."[24] In 1950, the One Nation group of Conservatives, influential in shaping the Conservative response to the welfare state, proclaimed, "The wall of social security has been built at last. Here and there stones need shifting or strengthening, here and there we could build better or more economical." Conservatives, however, should focus on "making the Welfare State work."[25]

Conservative governments between 1951 and 1964 kept this promise. Although the Conservatives did return the iron, steel, and trucking industries to private ownership, they left the bulk of Labour's nationalization program intact. They worked not to dismantle but to strengthen the National Health Service and undertook to guarantee full employment through Keynesian demand management and trade union negotiations. Spending on housing and education soared. Rather than challenging or seeking to shatter the social democratic consensus, Conservatives asserted their ideological claim to social democracy by recalling the paternalist roots of the party. As Conservatism had taken shape in the nineteenth century, it had translated the traditions of a hierarchical social order, of those on top of society caring for those on the bottom, into an embrace of state intervention to improve the lot of the poor. Thus, Anthony Eden (prime minister from 1955 to 1957) asserted, "We are not a party of unbridled, brutal capitalism, and never have been. Although we believe in personal responsibility and personal initiative in business, we are not the political children of the laissez-faire school."[26]

Margaret Thatcher, however, *was* a political child of the laissez-faire school. Unlike party leaders such as Eden, his successor Harold Macmillan, and even her beloved Churchill, Thatcher's vision of Conservatism did not include the ideals of noblesse oblige that allowed these men from upper-class backgrounds to accept social democracy. Her Dartford campaigns in 1949 and 1950—when she had no chance of winning and so had more freedom to say what she wanted than later during her years as junior minister—revealed her mistrust of social democracy and her instinctive economic liberalism. In these early speeches, Thatcher denounced high taxation rates as a disincentive to production and expressed hostility to the Labour government's nationalization program: "You cannot have the dream of building up your own fortune by your own hopes, your own hands and your own British guts." She condemned the various welfare provisions set into place by the postwar Labour Government as "pernicious" because, she warned, they "nibble into our national character far further than one would be aware at first glance."[27]At the core of her criticisms lay the liberal assumption that public policy should foster and protect individual initiative over social or state provision, and that the state-sponsored welfare programs could only undermine Britain's economic strength and weaken its social values.

Once Thatcher entered Parliament, however, she buried her dislike of the prevailing political consensus beneath her political ambition. When she had been campaigning in Dartford in 1949 and 1950, the Labour Government was still in the midst of the transition from wartime controls to Keynesian management of the economy, the public boards that would run the new nationalized industries had just been established, and most of the key provisions of the welfare state had just been enacted. The National Health Service, for example, was for many still an unknown, and frightening, entity. In contrast, by 1959, the social democratic settlement was just that: settled. By 1959, Britons regarded decent medical care, free at the point of service, as a right of citizenship and viewed the National Health Service as a beloved British institution and a source of national pride. Harold Macmillan, the Conservative prime minister from 1957, advocated the mixed economy and the welfare state with as much conviction as anyone on the Labour side of the House of Commons and so, too, did most members of his government.

Determined and intelligent, Thatcher followed the party line. She endorsed cooperation with the trade unions, backed the party's commitment to ensuring full employment through economic regulation and public investment, and pointed with pride to the Conservative record of increased public spending on housing, schools, and hospitals. During her three years as junior minister of Pensions and National Insurance—the government department most centrally concerned with administering the welfare state—she did prove herself to be Alfred Roberts's daughter in that her chief concern lay with the taxpayer rather than the beneficiaries of government relief, even when it meant opposing Christmas bonuses and supplemental payments to assist with the cost of heating in the winter months for pensioners (elderly retirees who lived only on their government pension). In general, though, Thatcher did little that set her apart from the social democratic mainstream. Most political observers saw her as largely middle of the road—"of the right, but not excessively so," in the words of one of her colleagues[28]—and a doer rather than a thinker, a practical politician with little interest in ideas.

Nevertheless, Thatcher's instinctive rejection of the social democratic consensus was never far from the surface. During the second half of the 1960s, with a Labour government now in office, her genuine convictions began to protrude more and more.

As Shadow Minister for both Power and Transport, her main areas of concern were nationalized industries—coal, gas, electricity, British Rail, and British Airways. During these years, her biographer John Campbell asserts, "Every speech, every utterance, that Mrs. Thatcher made ... shows her developing ever more clearly the conviction that public ownership was economically, politically and morally wrong."[29] She began to associate more and more with the Institute of Economic Affairs (IEA), a think tank established in 1957 to promote economic liberalism. In a series of speeches and articles, she also began to frame what would become one of the key planks of the Thatcherist platform: that political consensus simply meant a lack of firm political conviction.

At the same time, a Thatcherist constituency was beginning to take shape. Year after year at the annual Conservative Party conferences, throughout the 1950s and 1960s, representatives offered motions demanding that the postwar Labour Government's radical reforms be repealed. Although always defeated, these motions indicated that many in the Conservative rank and file had not embraced social democracy. Outside the party itself, a number of protest organizations and movements also articulated uneasiness with and, in many cases, an outright rejection of the social democratic settlement. Groups with names such as the Middle Class Alliance and the People's League for Defence of Freedom fought on a wide range of fronts for lower taxes, the rollback of welfare benefits, and the restriction of trade union power. Unlike the men who dominated the Conservative Party leadership and who tended to come from upper-class or upper-middle-class backgrounds, Thatcher understood the fears and resentments of the constituents of these organizations, voters in the lower-middle and "middle-middle" classes. She often described them as "our own people" and increasingly sought to align the Conservative Party with their interests. For Thatcher, "middle class" was not "simply a matter of income, but a whole attitude to life, a will to take responsibility for oneself."[30] Thatcher's people were "the millions of people who spend what they earn, not what other people earn. Who make sacrifices for their young family or their elderly parents . . . The sort of people I grew up with."[31]

In the 1960s, many of "our people" reacted with anger and confusion to their country's shifting position in the world and to accelerating social and cultural change at home. Three developments in particular—the disintegration of the British Empire, Britain's relative economic decline, and the rise of the "permissive society"—created a widening sense of national crisis among certain social sectors and helped prepare the ground for Thatcherism.

As the cold war polarized the world's states into two camps dominated by the capitalist and democratic United States and the Communist and dictatorial Soviet Union, British governments found their room for independent maneuver increasingly restricted. Until the end of the 1950s, both Labour and the Conservatives hoped that the Empire would guarantee British governments continuing clout in global affairs. In the words of Ernest Bevin, foreign secretary for Labour governments from 1945 to 1951, empire provided the means "to develop our own power and influence to equal that of the U.S. of A. and the U.S.S.R."[32] Pressure from nationalist independence movements, however, overwhelmed Britain's dwindling economic and military resources. The British pulled out of the Indian subcontinent and Palestine in the late 1940s, but the full-scale retreat from empire began in the late 1950s. Once the Gold Coast moved into independence as Ghana in 1957, decolonization proceeded at a breathless pace. By the end of the 1960s, the British Empire comprised little more than Gibraltar, Hong Kong, and a sprinkling of small island holdings. As early as 1961, Britain, which had once ruled the waves, possessed a total naval strength only one-sixth as large as that of the United States and one-fifth as large as that of the Soviet Union.

How much, though, did the empire matter to ordinary Britons? It seems reasonable to assume that on a day-to-day level, full employment, rising real wages, and access to decent health care mattered far more to most people than did the withdrawal of British troops from a host of African and Asian countries. But it is also reasonable to assume that many Britons, particularly those who had experienced World War II, found the sudden disintegration of the British Empire and the sharp reduction in Britain's global preeminence a confusing and disconcerting change. They had grown up regarding the empire as a given, and suddenly it was gone. Throughout the 1960s, then, British newspapers were "full of laments for Britain's lost greatness."[33]

This sense of lost greatness drew further sustenance from a growing awareness of Britain's relative economic decline. We have seen that ordinary British citizens experienced the 1950s and 1960s as the age of affluence; as Prime Minister Harold Macmillan proclaimed at the end of the 1950s, "Most of our people have never had it so good." But the consumer abundance of this era could not mask the fact that Britain was steadily falling behind its continental competitors in key economic indices. In 1950, for example, Britain stood in seventh place in a table of economic performance based on gross domestic product (GDP). By 1960, it had slipped to ninth; by 1970, to eighteenth. Britain's economy grew during these years, and at a healthy enough pace to sustain mass affluence, but its growth rates looked anemic compared to those of its European competitors. Between 1954 and 1977, West Germany saw its GDP rise by 310 percent and France by 297 percent, whereas the UK's growth in GDP hit only 75 percent.

A number of factors contributed to this relative economic decline. First, a long history of poor industrial relations limited British rates of productivity. Neither the nationalization of key industries nor the corporatist inclusion of trade union leaders in decision making had been able to overcome decades of hostility between workers and management. Second, throughout these years, Britain's military expenditures were far higher than most of its continental competitors, a legacy of its far-flung empire and the reluctance of British governments, both Conservative and

Labour, to accept a reduced role in world affairs. And third, both Labour and Conservative leaders in this era remained committed to propping up the value of the British pound sterling to maintain its position as an international reserve currency. With the pound overvalued on world markets, the price tag on British goods was higher than it should have been and so British exporters had trouble selling their goods abroad.

As a result of these factors, the British economy, even during the heyday of the Age of Affluence, was structurally unsound. With British consumers gobbling up imports at a voracious rate while British exporters struggled to find markets, the British economy faced recurrent "balance-of-payments crises"; that is, Britain could not pay the bill for its imports. Every balance-of-payments crisis made holders of the pound sterling around the world increasingly prone to trade their holdings for gold or other currencies—and every such "run on sterling" threatened the value of the British pound. British governments played a constant game of teeter-totter, pushing the economy up with expansionist policies that led inexorably to more consumer spending, balance-of-payments problems, and threats to the value of the pound, and then pressing the economy back down with deflationary policies designed to restrict imports. In 1967, the Labour government was forced to devalue the pound—a dramatic step that seemed to underscore Britain's relative economic decline.

Many British men and women linked their perception of Britain's declining global and economic position to their sense of national *moral* decline. They focused their criticisms on what came to be called the "permissive society." The permissiveness of the 1960s is frequently exaggerated—as late as 1969, one-quarter of British men and two-thirds of British women were virgins on their wedding day[34]—but rates of premarital and extramarital sexual activity did rise significantly during this period. The amount of nudity, sex, and violence depicted in the press, in film, on stage, and on television also increased dramatically. In 1969, for example, the Australian entrepreneur Rupert Murdoch purchased one of Britain's national daily newspapers and remade it as the *Sun*, the quintessential British tabloid, characterized by racy banner headlines and the requisite "page 3 girl," a new topless woman every day. At the same time, British society became decidedly more secular. Church attendance had been declining for decades, but it was the 1960s that saw a dramatic drop in other markers of religious faith, including Sunday school attendance, infant baptism, adolescent confirmation, and religious weddings.

The social legislation of Harold Wilson's Labour government during the second half of the 1960s both reflected and reinforced the widespread sense that a cultural revolution was underway. Under the guidance of the Labour Home Secretary Roy Jenkins, Wilson's government passed a series of social reforms, including the abolition of capital punishment and the legalization of abortion and homosexuality in 1967, the end of theater censorship in 1968, and the easing of divorce law in 1969. Jenkins saw these changes in the context of the protection of individual liberty: "Let us be on the side of those who want people to be free to live their own lives, to make their own mistakes, and to decide, in an adult way and provided they do not infringe on the rights of others, the code by which they wish to live."[35]

Jenkins's social legislation was popular among the "chattering classes": the educated elite who dominated politics, the universities, the BBC, and what the British refer to as the "quality press" (the highly respected London daily newspapers that shape elite opinion but are read by only a fraction of the British public). Many Britons, however, believed that this state-led cultural revolution had gone too far, too fast. With violent crime rates climbing—up by over 60 percent between 1967 and 1971[36]—they concluded that the reforms had ushered in not more freedom but more fear, and worried about a loss of moral authority and social cohesion.

The word "Thatcherism" was not coined until the mid-1970s; nevertheless, in the widening gap between popular and elite opinion during the 1960s, we can see Thatcherism beginning to emerge. Added together, the three significant developments traced earlier—the loss of empire, relative economic decline, and the advent of the permissive society—produced, by the end of the 1960s, a collective identity crisis, at least in the ranks of those that Thatcher regarded as "our people." For those men and women who found the loss of the old order threatening, Thatcherism promised not only renewed national strength and global power but also the restoration of law and order.

Thatcher herself regarded the Sixties not as a time of social liberation and cultural innovation but rather as "a world of make-believe," a failure of common sense and common decency.[37] Although a thorough-going economic liberal, Thatcher deplored the extension of liberal individualism into the sphere of social morality. In 1967, she voted in favor of legalizing abortion and homosexuality, but she later expressed ambivalence about her decisions: "matters did not turn out as was intended . . . [these reforms] paved the way towards a more callous, selfish and irresponsible society."[38] In her other votes, Thatcher showed that despite her Oxford education, she aligned firmly on the ordinary side of the ordinary people versus chattering classes divide. A firm advocate of the "short, sharp shock" of whipping convicted criminals, she had voted against her party leadership on the question of corporal punishment for juvenile criminals as far back as 1961.[39] In this she spoke for many of "our people." A poll in England in 1960 found 60 percent in favor of bringing back corporal punishment for certain crimes.[40]

Thatcher's advocacy of capital punishment was even more representative of a broad swathe of British public opinion. In 1965, the House of Commons abolished the death penalty for murder on a trial basis; this move was made permanent in 1969. Over the next two decades, thirteen Private Member's Bills (bills that ordinary MPs rather than the government introduce) attempted to restore capital punishment. Although surveys throughout the 1970s and 1980s showed that two-thirds of the British public favored bringing back the death penalty, every one of these bills went down to defeat. Thatcher explained how she voted on these bills in a television interview in 1984: "I personally have always voted for the death penalty because I believe that people who go out prepared to take the lives of other people forfeit their own right to live."[41]

Thatcher's rejection of the 1960s cultural revolution and her emphasis on law and order accorded with her vision of society as a larger version of her father's grocery store, a world where tidiness mattered and everything was in its proper place, where law-abiding, hard-working individuals could choose to spend the money they earned on products that would make their lives more comfortable. It was also a smart political choice. At the end of the 1960s, a married woman with children remained an oddity in British national political life (as it did throughout the Western world). Thatcher's sex made her a potentially threatening figure, a character with subversive potential; by aligning herself with law and order, Thatcher blunted her own edges. Extraordinary hard work, skillful self-presentation, and pragmatic politicking all ensured that she was well situated to take advantage of the collapse of political consensus in the 1970s.

CHAPTER 4

CRISIS, THE COLLAPSE OF CONSENSUS, AND THATCHER'S RISE TO THE TOP: 1970–1979

ON NOVEMBER 25, 1972, one of Britain's bestselling national daily newspapers branded Mrs. Thatcher "the most unpopular woman in Britain."[1] Less than seven years later, this most unpopular woman became Britain's prime minister. The decade of Thatcher's rise to power was a tumultuous time throughout the West, the period when terrorism became a global problem, and economic crisis became the order of the day. With inflation gutting their paychecks and their jobs in jeopardy, workers became restive. Strikes grew in numbers and violence. As social and political tensions escalated, the social democratic consensus shattered and democracy itself seemed vulnerable. The climate of crisis provided the opportunity for Thatcher to become leader of the Conservative Party in 1975 and then prime minister of Britain in 1979. As the first woman to lead a major Western political party, Thatcher was able to present herself as something new and to hold out the promise of a radical break with the present. Yet at the same time, she reassured voters that what she was offering was a return to a more stable, ordered, and powerful past.

In June 1970, Margaret Thatcher achieved her long-held ambition: She became a member of the British Cabinet. For the next four years she served as Secretary of the Department of Education in the Conservative government of Edward (Ted) Heath. Thatcher's sense of satisfaction at having achieved an important goal proved short-lived and she would later regard her role in the Heath government with embarrassment. She saw herself, for example, as the champion of the taxpayer and the proponent of reduced government spending, but as Education Secretary she became one of the biggest spenders in the government. Both the history of the Heath government and Thatcher's own record during this period reflected the wider confusion and contradictions of a political culture in crisis. The postwar political consensus, under strain during the 1960s, was beginning to collapse, but there was no agreement on how to restore what was collapsing or what could or should take its place.

Heath presented his government's election in 1970 as an important turning point in British politics: "We [the Conservatives] were returned to office to change the course of the history of this nation."[2] Like Thatcher, the new prime minister had risen from the lower middle class, through grammar school and Oxford, and up through the ranks of the Conservative Party. He came into office on a platform of industrial revitalization and economic modernization. To achieve these goals, he promised a number of radical changes, including Britain's entry into the European Community (or Common Market, the predecessor to the European Union), the replacement of Britain's antiquated shillings-farthings-and ha'pence currency by an up-to-date decimal system, and a new set of county boundaries for England. But most important, Heath promised to lead Britain in a new economic direction. He was determined, he said, to "leave more to individual or corporate effort . . . to encourage [men and women] more and more to take their own decisions, to stand firm on their own feet, to accept responsibility for themselves and their families."[3] Thus, he assured British voters that he would reduce the State's economic role and promised a partial retreat from Keynesian demand management and corporatism, two of the bastions of social democracy. More specifically, Heath pledged that his administration would no longer bail out failing industries or seek to manage the economy through wage and price limits negotiated with unions and business representatives.

Within less than two years, however, Heath authorized the financial bailout of one of Britain's large shipbuilding firms, declared a ninety-day statutory freeze on pay and prices, and returned to negotiating wages with union leaders. This "U-turn," as it has come to be known, was a response to devastating economic crisis. Less than a month after the election, a dock workers' strike shut down much of the British economy and forced Heath to declare a state of emergency. Then London garbage collectors and sewage plant workers walked off the job. Untreated sewage flowed into the Thames River and piles of trash rotted on the capital's streets. In December, electricity workers joined the picket lines. The resulting power outages forced the House of Commons to meet by candlelight, wreaked havoc in hospitals, tangled up traffic, and shut down assembly lines. Forced by power cuts to sit in the dark, Britons wondered if they had won World War II only to lose the peace. British economic growth rates, already lackluster in comparison to those on the continent, slowed even further and the specter of mass unemployment loomed. At the same time, inflation rates soared upward. Driving toward economic chaos, Heath took the U-turn. To save jobs, he ordered the shipbuilding bailout; trying to halt inflation, he froze wages and prices.

Thatcher and many other Conservatives came to regard Heath's U-turn as a cowardly retreat from the rigors of the free market to the false security of social democracy. The memory of the U-turn became pivotal in shaping Thatcherism over the next two decades, with the Heath government held up as the "could have, should have" moment in modern British history, a golden opportunity for fundamental change squandered because of

Heath's spinelessness. Looking back, Thatcher described the record of the Heath government as "indefensible."[4] At the time, however, she not only defended it, she saw no real alternative.

After reducing taxes and increasing pensions and other benefits—a classic Keynesian strategy—Heath was able to cut the unemployment numbers almost in half after his U-turn. Yet economic stability proved elusive. Inflation soared to an annual rate of 19 percent. The winter of 1973–1974 brought yet another miners' strike and Heath's fifth and longest state of emergency. Scrambling to cut fuel consumption, the government ordered the work week cut to three days and made it illegal to heat a factory, shop, or office. It also restricted the speed limit to 50 miles per hour and turned off television broadcasting at 10:30 pm. For a nation at peace, these measures were extraordinary, and extraordinarily unsettling. They also did little to restore investor confidence in the United Kingdom.

Heath blamed the unions for the economic disarray and warned that the massive strike actions threatened democracy itself. By causing chaos in the economy, he argued, unions ensured the failure of the elected government's policies and thus undermined the democratic process. The time had come, he insisted, for a showdown. At the beginning of 1974, Heath announced a general election and declared that if the Conservatives won, he would push through legislation to curb trade union power. Thus the election would be fought on the question, "Who rules Britain?"

The answer turned out to be, "Not you." No party won an overall majority. The Labour Party formed a minority government under Harold Wilson, and then consolidated its victory with a second general election just a few months later. Unfortunately, the change of government did little to halt Britain's economic slide. During the campaign, Wilson had promised to halt inflation, as well as the strikes that were ravaging the British economy, through a "social contract" between the government and the unions: Unions would moderate wage demands and rein in their members in exchange for higher governmental spending on social services. The whole idea of the social contract rested on an assumed partnership between the trade unions and the Labour Party, on the conviction that the unions would trust Labour, the party of the working class, to take care of their interests. But the social contract quickly collapsed. The Labour government found itself under almost immediate attack from Britain's old foes—a balance of payments crisis and the resulting international run on the pound. Struggling to shore up the currency and stabilize the economy, it announced cuts rather than expansions in social spending. From the unions' perspective, Labour had broken the social contract—and so the unions in turn abandoned their promises to rein in strikes and keep their wage demands low. By 1975, the unions were back on the picket lines, the inflation rate had hit 20 percent, the highest in western Europe, and the rate of unemployment was also climbing upward. People began to talk about "the British disease" and to wonder about Britain's economic viability.

Terrorism further intensified the crisis atmosphere as the sight of men, women, and children bleeding or blown apart on the streets of British cities began to appear on British television screens. This was the decade in which "The Troubles" in Northern Ireland exploded. During the 1960s, a nonviolent campaign to win civil rights for the Roman Catholic minority population of Northern Ireland had sparked a ferocious response from Protestant Unionists, who saw the campaign as nothing more than a front for anti-British Irish nationalism. Not only were Catholic neighborhoods under violent attack, but Northern Ireland's police force proved unable and largely unwilling to protect them. Out of this maelstrom came the revival of the Irish Republican Army—the IRA. These militants appointed themselves the protectors of Northern Irish Catholics. They also quickly transformed what had been a nonviolent civil rights movement into a nationalist war aiming at the destruction of the Union between Northern Ireland and Britain. British efforts to control the situation led the IRA to extend its terrorist activities to Britain itself and ushered in over thirty years of murder and mayhem across the United Kingdom.

A diary entry written by one of Wilson's political advisers at this time sums up the prevailing mood: "Britain is a miserable sight. A society of failures. . . . It is time to go and cultivate our gardens, share love with our families, and leave the rest to fester. And if it gets intolerable—because fascism could breed in this unhealthy climate—to emigrate if need be."[5] Many disillusioned Britons did choose to emigrate—throughout the first half of the 1970s emigrants outnumbered immigrants—and many more contemplated it, including Margaret and Denis Thatcher who considered sending their children to Canada. An editorial in the *Wall Street Journal* concluded, "Goodbye, Great Britain. It was nice knowing you," while on the CBS Evening News, the anchorman Eric Sevareid informed his viewers, "Britain is drifting slowly toward a condition of ungovernability."[6]

The sense of malaise and the fear of incipient anarchy were not, however, confined to Britain. In France at this time, for example, political theorists wrote of the "stalled" society, while an editorial in the influential Italian newspaper *La Stampa* warned in 1974 that "Italy . . . runs the risk of becoming a country on the outskirts of civilization and reason."[7] Terrorism became a global, not just a British, epidemic threat the 1970s. The radical protest movements of the 1960s had heightened expectations among many minority, nationalist, and political groups hoping for radical social change. By the early 1970s, many felt frustrated that their expectations had not been met. Some, then, gave up on the hope of achieving their goals through political persuasion and instead resorted to bombings, hijackings, and assassinations. ETA in Spain, the PLO in Israel and Palestine, Baader-Meinhof in Germany, the Red Brigades in Italy, and the Weathermen in the United States, as well as Ireland's IRA: the names differed, as did the motivations, but the pools of blood, the scattered body parts, the weeping family members, and the pervasive sense of fear seemed very much the same.

The turn toward terrorism is the most extreme example of the political disenchantment that characterized the 1970s across much of the West. This was the decade when the phenomenal economic growth of the post–World War II period suddenly halted and political leaders did not seem to know what to do about it. Double-digit inflation rates gutted family and national budgets and joblessness grew. By 1975, the average annual growth rate within western Europe nations had dropped to zero. As governments appeared helpless in the face of both terrorist attacks and economic disaster, political division grew sharper and social discontent grew. Across western Europe and the United States, voters scrambled to throw out the parties in charge and put their opponents in their place—and yet little changed. Unions demanded higher wages for their members who were struggling to keep pace with inflation, but higher wage settlements accelerated the climb of inflation rates. Political leaders who sought to limit such settlements faced massive, and often violent, strikes. In West Germany, for example, the strike rate in the 1970s stood at three times that of 1960s, with almost four times as many working days lost as a result. In Italy and France, worker unrest reached epidemic proportions and threatened the political stability of these states.

What was going on? How do we explain the end to the Age of Affluence and the fragmentation of the postwar social democratic political consensus? Part of the answer rests in a new term, coined for a new reality: *stagflation.* Before the 1970s, inflation and unemployment seemed to be mutually exclusive: robust economies featured little or no unemployment but tended toward inflation, while stagnant economies were devoid of inflation but suffered from high unemployment. The job of governments was to find the right balance to ensure healthy growth rates, low unemployment, and manageable inflation. The experience of the

1970s challenged these economic orthodoxies. The high unemployment rates of a stagnant economy had somehow combined with the escalating inflation numbers of an economy in overdrive. This unprecedented combination of high unemployment and high inflation—stagflation—spread political frustration and social disorder across western Europe and much of the world.

Explanations for stagflation often highlight the impact of the oil crisis. In October 1973, a coalition of Arab states invaded Israel in what became known as the Yom Kippur War. Angered by western support for Israel, Arab governments raised oil prices by 70 percent and imposed a temporary embargo on oil sales to the United States and western Europe. Oil prices rose fourfold almost overnight—"the most dramatic and economically damaging global price rise in history"—and inflation rippled through western economies.[8] And the prices kept climbing: by 1979, OPEC prices were ten times higher than they had been in 1973.

Yet oil alone did not account for stagflation. The oil crisis only accelerated a systemic shift already underway in western economies: the move from industrialism to *postindustrialism*. This shift meant the disappearance of high-paying and dependable jobs in the heavy extractive and manufacturing industries. Coal ceased to be the engine of economic life, replaced by oil, natural gas, and nuclear power. Manufacturing migrated to developing economies in Asia and South America, where lower wage rates and fewer workers' rights ensured higher corporate profits. In those factories and plants that remained in the West, industrial processes grew more mechanized. Jobs in these places thus tended to be not only fewer but less-skilled and lower-paying, often part-time and increasingly filled by women. The same pattern held true in the expanding, often nonunionized service sector of the economy. For workers throughout the West, then—particularly male workers without advanced education in industrial occupations—the 1970s meant contracting economic opportunity and blocked expectations.

Significantly, the word "stagflation" was coined not in 1974 or 1975, but in 1965, and in Britain. In November of 1965, the Conservative Party economic spokesman Iain Macleod criticized the Labour government with a prescient speech. Macleod said, "We now have the worst of both worlds—not just inflation on the one side or stagnation on the other, but both of them together. We have a sort of 'stagflation' situation."[9] Well before the oil crisis hit, then, the British economy was displaying the signs of stagnancy that would characterize much of western Europe by the mid-1970s. As Britain was the first nation in the world to industrialize, perhaps it is not surprising that it was the first to experience the painful transition to postindustrialism. In Britain in the 1950s, 690,000 men delved in coal mines; by the early 1980s, this number had dropped to 60,000. Over 48 percent of the British workforce was employed in the industrial sector in the 1950s but only 29 percent by the 1980s. No other western European country experienced such a rapid industrial decline. An entire way of life was changing. In the industrial unrest that so marked the 1970s in Britain, we can see people, hurt by this change, fighting to preserve the only way of life they had known, a way of life that had brought them unprecedented prosperity but that now was disappearing along with that prosperity.

In this tumultuous climate, Thatcher climbed to the top of the British Conservative Party. The fact that she did so shocked many of her own party members and in some ways seems to have shocked Thatcher herself. Shortly before deciding to stand in the leadership election she told a television interviewer that she did not think that "the country is ready to have a woman leader."[10] Certainly not many people in the early 1970s would have predicted that Thatcher would be that woman. As Education Secretary in Heath's troubled government from 1970 to 1974, she did not possess a great deal of power (which helps explain why Education was considered a woman's job, unlike the position of Foreign Secretary or the Chancellor of the Exchequer). She did,

NEAR THE TOP. *Thatcher makes a point at the Conservative Party Conference in October 1974. Behind her is party leader Edward Heath.*

however, achieve every politician's dream of becoming a house-hold name—unfortunately as "the lady nobody loves."[11]

Thatcher's national notoriety resulted from her desire to cut costs in the primary school budget in order to free up funds for the Open University, an innovative distance learning and re-search institution set up in 1971. The end was worthy but many British parents found the means to that end less so. In 1972, Thatcher announced that children in primary schools would no longer receive milk for free. Instead, families with incomes above a set level would have to pay if they wished their children to drink milk in the classroom. The policy shift proved immensely contro-versial. It gave rise to the unforgettable phrase "Mrs. Thatcher, Milk-Snatcher" and resulted in Thatcher being labeled "the most unpopular woman in Britain."[12] The months that followed were some of the worst of her long political career. The School Milk Act of 1946, which required all schools to provide one-third pint of milk free to all pupils, was part of the legislative foundations of the postwar welfare state. To many Britons, free school milk represented the best of social democracy, a symbol of its communal values and of the ideal of social citizenship. They thus responded in absolute fury to Thatcher's move.

Yet the sense of dismay at the crumbling of postwar social citizenship was not the only factor in play in the milk-snatcher controversy. Just four years earlier, when the Labour Education Secretary Edward Short declared that secondary school pupils would no longer receive free milk, he encountered some opposition, but nothing along the lines of the uproar that greeted Thatcher's decision. Unlike Short, Thatcher was a woman, and a woman who decided to stop providing milk to little children (rather than secondary-school teenagers). Thatcher's action thus transgressed against deeply rooted gender assumptions. Opponents attacked her person as well as her policy, and questioned her not only as a politician but as a *mother*. Milk snatching, in this rhetoric, signaled that Thatcher was unnatural, deficient somehow in maternal instinct and thus lacking as a woman as well as a political leader. Forced to compromise, she restored free milk to children under age seven.

Thatcher survived the controversy, but the episode demonstrated how crucial it was for her to control her public image. It also revealed the peril of gender politics. Thatcher had long capitalized on her sex, manipulating female stereotypes to present herself to voters as authoritative yet nonthreatening, and using the novelty of women in public office to attract publicity and grab plum jobs. With the milk-snatcher cry, however, her opponents showed how easy it was to deploy gender as a weapon against her. Her time in Education convinced Thatcher to redefine her own approach to politics and in the process, to reset the perimeters of a woman's job.

Thatcher emerged as the Conservative Party Leader just three years after the milk-snatcher controversy through a somewhat strange sequence of events. A change in parliamentary party rules meant that for the first time ever, Conservative MPs could run against the existing leader for the position. Thus, when Heath refused to step down after the general election defeat in 1974, the way was clear for a leadership contest within the party. Confronted with the brave new world of party democracy, however, high-ranking Conservatives dithered. The favored candidate to replace Heath refused to run against his leader. This display of traditional deference gave the relatively young and definitely female Thatcher a surprising opportunity. She ran as a kind of stalking horse, widely expected not to win but to get enough votes to humiliate Heath and force him to step aside for a more established (and male) Conservative. Instead, Thatcher *won*, even though almost every single member of the Conservative Shadow Cabinet openly opposed her.

What no one—perhaps not even Thatcher—seemed to have realized was the depth of discontent among ordinary MPs. These "backbenchers" rarely made public speeches and usually voted as they were told, but they were now fed up, fearful, and ready for a drastic change. Thatcher became that change. No woman had ever before led a major political party in the West. As so often in her career, Thatcher transformed what could have been the

DAILY EXPRESS CARTOON: ST JOAN MARGARET. *In the guise of St. Joan of Arc, Thatcher leads her Conservative troops into battle against Labour Prime Minister Harold Wilson.*

liability of her sex into an advantage. She had little to offer yet in terms of specific plans or policies, but what she did have to offer was the promise that things would change—which her very body made clear.

At the same time, Thatcher recognized that many MPs were uncomfortable with the idea of a woman leader and so she reassured them by painting herself in comforting colors. She made sure, for example, that reporters accompanied her to the grocery store and that the cameras caught her making breakfast for Denis on the day of the election. "I am," she told not only MPs but the British public, "a very ordinary person who leads a very normal life . . . shopping keeps me in touch."[13] The Labour MP Barbara Castle, herself very familiar with the complex negotiations involved in being a female politician in Britain, noted, "Margaret's election has stirred up her own side wonderfully; all her backbenchers perform like knights jousting at a tourney for a lady's favours."[14] Thatcher played her part in this new tournament skillfully. Few Conservative MPs had known her very well before 1975; a workaholic and a woman with a family, she had never been one to spend much time with colleagues over lunches or drinks. After Thatcher became Leader, however, she spent more time with the backbenchers—her power base—than had any previous Conservative prime minister. And she did so in a reassuringly womanly way: she asked after spouses, children, and grandchildren; she paid attention to birthdays and bereavements; she fussed and even flirted.

Once Thatcher had won over the Conservative backbenchers in the parliamentary party, she faced the task of winning over enough of the British public to ensure a Conservative victory in the next general election. As part of this project, she revised her public image. With the help of the former television producer Gordon Reece, Thatcher filed down the upper-class edges that she had developed in her years of marriage. She abandoned hats, moderated her jewelry, and worked with a voice coach both to lower her voice (so that she would sound less shrill in parliamentary debates) and to downgrade her accent (so that she would sound more ordinary). It was during this period that Thatcher began to exaggerate the poverty of her upbringing with a public narrative that featured her grocer father and the corner shop in Grantham rather than her millionaire husband and the enormous country house in Kent. Reese also convinced Thatcher to shift her focus from the "quality press"—the London daily newspapers—and instead to concentrate her efforts on the popular tabloids, women's magazines, and light entertainment radio and television programs. One observer labeled this image makeover "Maggification," a reference to "Maggie," the name that tabloid headline writers bestowed on Mrs. Thatcher.[15] A distinctly lower-class nickname, Maggie was not a name that any of Thatcher's family members used, but it suited her new public image to perfection.

Maggie was not, however, a complete fiction. The social changes of the 1960s had created a wide gap between the political and cultural elite and many middle- and working-class Britons. Despite her education and achievements, Thatcher placed herself firmly on the ordinary side of that gap. With the party leadership secure, she now moved into a role that came utterly naturally for her: she became a populist politician. She voiced the longings and fears of those she frequently called "our people," upper-working-class and lower-middle-class homeowners and aspiring homeowners who felt alienated by the cultural changes underway since the 1960s and who looked back with longing toward what they perceived to be a more orderly, disciplined world.

Thatcher's promise of a more orderly society was especially appealing after the disorientation of the Heath years. Although a Conservative, Heath was not conservative; he was instead a modernizer, someone who sought to clear out what he saw as outdated and inefficient traditions, to standardize, to rationalize, to centralize. As Thatcher recalled (rather sardonically), "There was to be a clean break and a fresh start and new brooms galore."[16] Many people resented the way that Heath's new brooms swept aside much that was familiar. Decimalization, for example, meant a change in something as quotidian as the coins in a person's pockets. Similarly, Heath's sweeping reorganization of local government not only replaced 800 local councils with much larger units, but also redrew the centuries-old county map of England. Residents of Rutland, England's smallest county, suddenly found themselves living in Leicestershire; Yorkshiremen in the southwestern portion of this proud region discovered they now belonged to something called Humberside. Intended to cut costs and improve the delivery of services, these reforms replaced the familiar and the local with new, bigger, less accessible, more bureaucratic structures. Once in office, Thatcher would continue Heath's emphasis on centralization and standardization. Nevertheless, she successfully presented herself during the 1970s and long after as a true conservative, as someone whose principal aim was to conserve traditional British values and a distinctly British way of life for "our people."

Thatcher's increasing emphasis on traditional gender roles resonated with British men and women who found themselves disoriented by the cultural changes they saw around them and desperate to shore up what they saw as endangered traditional boundaries. In the 1950s, Thatcher had urged married women with children to embrace careers, but she now insisted that it was best for children and families if mothers stayed home. Increasingly, she began to point to the working mother as the source of rising juvenile crime and wider social breakdown. Feminists who hailed her rise to the party leadership as an advance for their cause soon found themselves disabused. Thatcher rejected the feminist label, saw no reason for any sort of antidiscrimination legislation, and famously said of the women's liberation movement, "What has it ever done for me?"[17] She played up her experience as a mother and a homemaker, and emphasized the ways in which these identities fitted her to serve as the spokesperson for "our people."

The emphasis on "our people," however, carried an implicit contrast: *our* people versus those who were not us, but *them*. Many of Thatcher's supporters were attracted not only by her themes of inclusion—one of us, our people, our way of life—but also by the implied exclusion of others. Thatcher was not a racist but she believed that to be British was to be white. Her belief in the greatness of the British Empire did not translate into any sense of national or imperial kinship with the people of color who had made up most of the population of that empire. She had little interest in or attachment to the Commonwealth, the loose organization of states that had once been in the British Empire. A speech to her Finchley constituents in 1961 made clear her perspective: "Many of us do not feel quite the same allegiance to Archbishop Makarios or Doctor Nkrumah or to people like Jomo Kenyatta [leaders of newly independent Cyprus, Ghana, and Kenya] as we do towards Mr. Menzies [the firmly pro-British prime minister] of Australia."[18]

As much as Thatcher would have liked to ignore the Commonwealth, however, she could not. In the post–World War II era, Jamaicans, Indians, Pakistanis, and other migrants from Commonwealth countries and colonies headed to what they had been taught to think of as the "Mother Country." This coloring of British society was part of a larger movement of non-white, non-Western populations into western Europe. Pushed in some cases by decolonization and pulled in almost all cases by the promise of jobs in booming economies, immigrants from African, Asian, Caribbean, and Middle Eastern states began to migrate to Europe in ever-increasing numbers in the 1950s and 1960s. They flowed into jobs in heavy industrial regions, as well as the expanding welfare sector, which heavily depended on low-wage immigrant employees. In Britain, industrial cities in the Midlands and North, such as Birmingham and Bradford, rapidly became home to an expanding population of color. By 1970, 450,000 migrants from the West Indians (the majority from Jamaica), 119,000 from Pakistan, and 270,000 from India had made their home in Britain.

Confined by poor wages and systematic discrimination to substandard housing in crumbling neighborhoods, these immigrant groups encountered hostility from many of their neighbors. Despite a century of propaganda that aimed to foster a sense of common imperial identity, few white Britons regarded non-white immigrants as British. Many instead linked the growing non-white populations to rising levels of crime and to a more general sense of disorder and disintegration. The end of the 1950s saw race riots in London and Nottingham; the openly racist British National Party formed in 1960 and, in 1967, amalgamated with other racist groups in the National Front. Responding to white unease, both Conservative and Labour governments in the 1960s passed legislation that sought, on the one hand, to limit the entry of migrants from the West Indies, Africa, and the Indian subcontinent while on the other hand, to keep open the population flow of white Britons to and from the "white Commonwealth" of Australia, New Zealand, and Canada.

The economic downturn of the 1970s, particularly the rising unemployment rates, exacerbated racial tensions in Britain (and throughout western Europe). No economist could explain stagflation, but anyone could point to a Caribbean or Asian immigrant on the factory floor or behind the shop counter and argue (wrongly) that there was the cause of white unemployment. Immigrants of color made easy scapegoats: readily identifiable, concentrated in certain neighborhoods, economically vulnerable. Economic fear and racial anxieties thus found an outlet in protests against immigration. Politicians quickly responded. Across Europe, governments reacted to rising unemployment rates by endeavoring to halt mass immigration.

In the United Kingdom, Heath's Conservative government passed the Immigration Act of 1971, crafted in such a way that it specifically and intentionally banned the immigration of people of color while easing entry into the UK for whites. It did so with the concept of the "patrial." A patrial was someone with a parent or grandparent born in or a citizen of the United Kingdom; according to the 1971 law, patrials—almost all of them white—were not subject to immigration control. Other imperial and

Commonwealth citizens—almost all of them not white—now found their access to Britain largely blocked. (In addition, the act made sure that immigrants from the Republic of Ireland—again, almost exclusively white—were not subject to controls.)

Thatcher supported this legislation, as she had supported previous efforts to limit the immigration of people of color. Here again her instincts were those of a populist, as she revealed in her response to what became known as the "Rivers of Blood" controversy in 1968. The controversy erupted because of a speech—now one of the most famous political speeches in British history—given by Enoch Powell, a prominent Conservative MP and member of the Shadow Cabinet alongside Thatcher. Convinced that Britain was in peril, Powell invited reporters to a meeting he was holding with his constituents in Birmingham, where he delivered a deliberately incendiary speech. Quoting a letter written by one of his voters, Powell warned that "'in fifteen or twenty years' time the black man will have the whip hand over the white man.'" Ramping up the rhetoric, he declared, "Those whom the gods wish to destroy, they first make mad. We must be mad, literally mad." Sanity could only be restored, Powell believed, by banning non-white immigration and instituting a massive program of voluntary repatriation of non-whites already in Britain. He concluded by citing the ancient Roman poet Virgil: "Like the Roman, I seem to see 'the River Tiber foaming with much blood.'"[19] Most of his listeners would not have gotten the reference to the *Aeneid*, but they understood his point: that a multiracial Britain would be a violent Britain.

The Rivers of Blood speech sparked a political firestorm. Powell's parliamentary colleagues were horrified. It violated the boundaries of British decency and seemed a conscious attempt to stoke racist rage. Conservative Party leader Edward Heath condemned the speech and dismissed Powell from the Shadow Cabinet. Powell would never again hold high office. But at the same time that the speech condemned Powell to the parliamentary sidelines, it also made him one of the most popular politicians in

Britain: over 100,000 supportive letters and postcards poured into Powell's office in the days after the speech. Opinion polls showed that over 70 percent of those surveyed agreed with Powell's stand against a multiracial society.[20]

One of those who agreed—but quietly—was Margaret Thatcher. She "strongly sympathized" with Powell's anti-immigration line and—in private—opposed Heath's decision to remove Powell from the Shadow Cabinet.[21] Like Powell, she believed that the *mixing* of cultures almost guaranteed the *clashing* of cultures and hence that multiculturalism threatened national cohesion. Thatcher and Powell were not close, even though they both sat in the Shadow Cabinet in the late 1960s and agreed on many issues, including this one. Powell's well-known horror at the presence of women in political life contributed to the frostiness of their political relationship, but so, too, did Thatcher's well-honed political sense. Thatcher played a much more skillful and pragmatic political game. Not until she became Conservative leader did she articulate popular discomfort with immigration and its multicultural consequences, and when she did so, she used carefully coded language. In a much-publicized interview, Thatcher asserted, "We are a British nation with British characteristics . . . People are really rather afraid that this country might be rather swamped by people with a different culture." Political leaders on both sides of the House condemned her for fomenting racial tensions—but the letters of support from ordinary voters came pouring in and Thatcher did not hesitate to repeat her popular line.[22]

Within the context of the 1970s, the Them-versus-Us way in which Thatcher saw the world cut through the complexities and offered clarity to British voters dismayed by Britain's apparent descent into economic and political anarchy. "Maggie," the commonsensical housewife, was a practical and reassuring figure who promised to brook no nonsense and to tidy things up in no time. But she was also an ardent British nationalist who did not hesitate to assert that Britain still had a leading role to play in global affairs. "We in the Conservative party believe that Britain is still great," she declared.[23] Here Maggie gave way to Britannia, the warrior leading her people into battle. Moreover, in foreign affairs as much as in domestic politics, Thatcher's preference for bipolarities offered a clear, clean, appealing vision.

Before becoming Conservative Party leader, Thatcher had rarely traveled outside Britain. Once she won the leadership election, however, she embarked on a series of foreign visits across the globe, in an effort not only to educate herself but also to polish her image as a strong and commanding leader. Already a source of media attention because of her position as the first female leader of a major Western political party, she soon became a global celebrity.

The Soviet leadership inadvertently assisted Thatcher in her quest to make a name for herself around the world. In 1976, Thatcher gave a speech focusing on the cold war at Kensington Town Hall in London. In remarkably forthright language for a politician, she condemned détente, the live-and-let-live policy, buttressed by arms reductions negotiations, that US President Richard Nixon had initiated in the late 1960s. Détente, Thatcher insisted, was just another word for appeasement and just as appeasement rested on a misjudgment of Hitler and his aims, so détente was driven by misconceptions about the Soviet Union. "The Russians are bent on world dominance," Thatcher warned.[24] The Soviets took the bait. In a public response to Thatcher's speech, they derided her claims as paranoia and contemptuously labeled her the "Iron Lady." The insult delighted her. At a formal dinner with her constituents a few days later, Thatcher appropriated the label: "Ladies and Gentlemen, I stand before you tonight in my green chiffon evening gown, my face softly made up, my fair hair gently waved . . . The Iron Lady of the Western World. Me? A cold warrior? . . . Well, yes, if that is how they wish to interpret my defence of values and freedoms fundamental to our way of life."[25]

The worldwide publicity surrounding the Iron Lady speech was a godsend to an aspiring prime minister. Thatcher had thrust herself into the ranks of People Who Matter; more than that, she had staked out her turf as a cold warrior. It was familiar ground for her. In Thatcher's Them-versus-Us view of the world, Soviet-style communism had long constituted the ultimate Them. She firmly believed that communism was a force of un-adulterated evil, that only the West's superiority in nuclear capa-bility kept the peace, and thus that the arms control negotiations that undergirded détente, although well-intentioned, threatened that peace.

Thatcher, however, did not preach doom and gloom. Part of her appeal lay in her extraordinary confidence and in her upbeat message. At the same time that Thatcher charged that détente un-derestimated the Soviet threat by failing to see that the Soviets were bent on world domination, she also insisted that détente *overestimated* the Soviets. The policy of détente assumed that the cold war was unwinnable and that therefore some kind of negoti-ated truce was essential. Such defeatism was nonsense, Thatcher contended. Economically, politically, and morally unsustainable, communism would collapse—provided that the West main-tained its superiority in values and in military strength.

Domestic politics, of course, consumed far more of Thatcher's time than did foreign affairs during her time as Leader of the Opposition, but Thatcher tended to view her struggle against the social democratic consensus at home as part and parcel of the wider Western battle against global communism. She refused to acknowledge social democracy as a Western political system distinct from that of the Soviet-dominated states of Eastern Europe. If left in office, she warned, the Labour government would lead Britain by "rapid strides toward the Iron Curtain state."[26] To drive that message home, Thatcher almost always called her Labour opponents socialists. In a typical speech in 1976, for example, she asserted, "Our aim is not just to remove a uniquely incompetent Government from office. It is to destroy the whole fallacy of socialism that the Labour Party exists to spread."[27] She presented Thatcherism (a word first used shortly after she won the leadership election) as "a crusade not merely to put a temporary brake on Socialism, but to stop its onward march once and for all."[28]

Thatcherism took shape in these years against a background of rising inflation. We have seen that Thatcher inherited the classical liberal ideals of her father: the belief that an individual's political liberty depended on economic liberty, on the right to buy and sell goods and services on the free market and to acquire—or lose—private property. This emphasis on individual freedom led Thatcher, once she became party leader, to identify inflation as a threat to democracy as well as prosperity. "Inflation," she declared, "destroys nations and societies as surely as invading armies do."[29] By reducing the value of the money in an individual's pocket or savings account, inflation restricted individual options and thus constituted an infringement of personal freedom. In addition, Thatcher argued, inflation particularly hurt those individuals with whom she most identified—our people—the thrifty middle-class folks who "put something by and then in fact find that it won't buy what they thought it would when they saved the money up in the first place." The result, in Thatcher's view, was *moral* as well as economic disaster. Inflation "destroyed the faith of many people in some of our traditional ways of life, in being independent, in being thrifty and saving for a rainy day."[30]

In identifying inflation rather than the rising unemployment rate as the enemy, Thatcher broke sharply with the postwar political consensus. As we have seen, the memory of the mass unemployment of the 1930s loomed large in British politics after World War II. At the core of the consensus was the agreement that it was the job of the British government to ensure full employment. The climbing jobless rate of the 1970s was for most Britons absolutely horrifying, a betrayal of the basic assumption on which they had rebuilt their society after total war. Thatcher certainly recognized this fact, and used it to score political points against the Labour government. One of her most famous party propaganda pieces was a billboard sign featuring a photograph of a lengthy line of jobseekers outside the Unemployment Office with the headline "Labour Isn't Working." (The photo was staged; the men and women turned out to be Conservative Party activists who lined up for the shot.) Yet in private conversations and planning sessions, Thatcher and her advisors were willing to shrug off high unemployment as a risk worth taking in order to tackle inflation. In one strategy session, for example, they discussed how "unemployment in the 1970s would be (or could be made) less unpalatable than unemployment in the past."[31]

Thatcher's emphasis on inflation over unemployment reflected the ideas of the controversial economists Friedrich Hayek and Milton Friedman. Although they differed on key issues, Hayek (an Austrian who lived during the 1940s in England) and Friedman (an American) agreed on a very basic point: John Maynard Keynes was wrong. More specifically, they rejected Keynes's argument that in a capitalist democracy, the central state can and must use the tools at its disposal to ensure continued economic growth and thus maintain full employment. While Hayek was profoundly skeptical of the ability of political leaders to understand and therefore regulate complex economies, Friedman did allot an economic policymaking role to government. In place of Keynesian theories of demand management, he offered what came to be known as *monetarism*. In brief, monetarists like Friedman insisted that inflation, not unemployment, posed the greatest danger to capitalist prosperity and that the money supply, not wages or prices, determined inflation.

In the wake of the disasters of the Heath years, monetarist ideas and a more general dissatisfaction with the Keynesian ideal of an economically activist state began to gain adherents in Britain and particularly in the Conservative Party. Thatcher was not the only Conservative who became convinced that the party had lost its way and that the social democratic political consensus needed to be jettisoned. "Keynes is dead," announced one Conservative economic advisor.[32] Prominent Conservative intellectuals such as Keith Joseph, the man who Thatcher always acknowledged as her mentor and to whom she dedicated her autobiography, began to argue that it was time to abandon the commitment to full employment and, instead, to focus on monetary policy in order to reduce inflation. "Inflation is threatening to destroy society," Joseph warned.[33] Thatcher herself insisted, "Before I ever read a page of Milton Friedman . . . I just knew that [Keynes'] assertions could not be true."[34] Monetarism, however, gave Thatcherism intellectual clout. Although not much of an original thinker, Thatcher was the consummate politician, with an extraordinary ability to consume the ideas of others and repackage them for a mass audience.

In speech after speech, interview after interview from 1975 on, Thatcher built on the monetarist critique of Keynesianism to assail the entire social democratic political consensus. Economics and morality were linked, she insisted. "The economic success of the Western world," she warned, "is a product of its moral philosophy and practice." In Thatcher's reading of history, western European culture (and its outposts in the United States, Canada, Australia, and New Zealand) rested on faith in the individual's freedom of choice. Any limits on individual choice—and on the individual's responsibility to face the consequences of those choices—undercut the ethical foundations of a free society. "The sense of being self-reliant . . . of owning one's own property, of paying one's way," she argued, "are all part of the spiritual ballast which maintains responsible citizenship."[35] The growth of state welfare programs thus constituted an ethical threat as well as economic burden. If the state takes the place of charitable and voluntary action, "you will begin to deprive human beings of one of the essential ingredients of humanity—personal moral responsibility. You will in effect dry up in them the milk of human kindness."[36] State action to promote equality would lead not to a more just and equitable society, but instead, inevitably and inexorably, to "State control over people's lives."[37]

Thatcher's attack on the social democratic consensus grew in appeal as the 1970s advanced. By the end of the decade, an increasing number of British men and women on the Left and the Right agreed that fundamental questions had to be asked as the once-solid certainties of the postwar order eroded and as British economic decline continued. In 1976, pressure on the British pound from international currency speculators was so great that the prime minister, Labour leader James Callaghan, was forced to negotiate a loan from the International Monetary Fund (IMF)— the largest loan the IMF had proffered up to that point. In exchange for the bailout, the Labour government had to agree to slash spending. Speaking to the Labour Party conference shortly after the loan was finalized, Callaghan seemed to be announcing the death of Keynesianism and the birth of a new economic order: "We used to think that you could spend your way out of a recession and increase employment by cutting taxes and boosting government spending." Callaghan lamented the loss of "that cosy world" where "a stroke of the chancellor's pen" could guarantee full employment, but he warned, "I tell you in all candour that that option no longer exists."[38]

Many Britons regarded the IMF loan as a national humiliation. One popular television presenter described Britain as "old and worn, on the brink of ruin, bankrupt in all but heritage and hope, and even those were in pawn."[39] For Thatcher, however, the loan and its conditions presented a different sort of problem. Under the loan's requirements, Callaghan's Labour government not only slashed spending and abandoned any plans for further industrial nationalization but also began to rein in the money supply—in other words, to pursue the sort of monetarist policies Thatcher advocated. It became more difficult for Thatcher to pin the socialist label on the Labour government when Callaghan was able to brag that "We have been attempting to live within our means after the profligate extravagance of the Conservative Government."[40] In 1977, both the rate of inflation and the number of strikes declined, as did Thatcher's popularity level in polls.

The biggest problem Thatcher faced was that voters associated a Conservative government with disaster. In particular, she knew that many people remembered Heath's catastrophic confrontations with the unions that had led to widespread power cuts and to the three-day workweek. Thatcher personally believed that corporatism granted unelected trade union leaders far too much political power and so infringed on the rights of individual workers (and bosses) at the same time that it interfered with the free market. Yet throughout the years that she led the party in opposition, Thatcher found herself having to reassure the electorate that Conservatives were not union bashers and that a Conservative government could be trusted to work with the unions for British prosperity. Hence, at the Conservative Party conference in 1976, Thatcher said, "Let me make it absolutely clear that the next Conservative Government will look forward to discussion and consultation with the trade union movement about the policies that are needed to save our country."[41] Thatcher, along with other members of her Shadow Cabinet, agreed with Conservative Party strategists that challenging the unions too aggressively would "risk losing the election in the subsequent rumpus."[42]

The dramatic events of 1979, however, made such bows to the corporatist consensus utterly unnecessary and cleared the way for Thatcher to win the next election. The year opened with bitter cold and abundant snow. A sudden thaw caused massive flooding, followed by more blizzards. Trade union action then created the perfect political storm. Drivers of oil tankers and delivery trucks went on strike, causing fuel shortages and triggering panic buying that left some areas short of food. In February, the first of what would be many public-sector employee strike actions began. Over the next several weeks, groups on strike included garbage collectors, hospital porters, school janitors, ambulance drivers, gravediggers, and crematorium workers. The "Winter of Discontent," as it came to be known (after the opening line of Shakespeare's *Richard III*), was underway. For many Britons, the unions, once the champions of society's victims, had now become the villains, greedy thugs who threatened the ill, refused to care for the injured, interfered with children's education, and let the dead lie unburied. The unpopularity of the unions reached unprecedented levels and even union members began to demand restrictions on trade union power. In one Gallup poll, 44 percent described the very existence of unions as "a bad thing."[43]

The winter's strikes worked in Thatcher's favor. First, they not only robbed the union movement of much of its moral appeal, they also undermined the Labour government's legitimacy. The Winter of Discontent catapulted Britons back to the Bad Old Days of the Heath years—but now a Labour government was in charge, a government whose very existence was presaged on its partnership with the trade unions and its promise to use that partnership to manage the economy effectively and to create a more just society. Second, the strikes liberated Thatcher politically; her instinctive contempt for the union movement could now be expressed as a form of patriotism. Speaking about the strikes to a radio audience, for example, she proclaimed, "If someone is confronting our essential liberties, if someone is inflicting injury, harm and damage on the sick, my God, I will confront them."[44] She charged that the Labour government had allowed "the rule of the mob" to replace the rule of law, and argued that only a Conservative administration could put things back in order.[45]

On March 28, 1979, the Labour government lost a vote of confidence in the House of Commons—something that had not happened in British politics since 1924. With the election set for May 4, Thatcher had a little over a month—a long campaign in British terms—to convince British voters that the time had come for Thatcherism. She did not offer many details about actual policies. Instead she focused on linking Labour to failed socialism and urging voters to cast their ballots for change.

As in her campaign for the Conservative Party leadership four years earlier, Thatcher used the fact of her femaleness to embody that change. In general, she viewed her sex as a positive campaign asset, something to be highlighted rather than hidden.

Her advisors did prevent her from debating Callaghan on television because of concerns about the gender implications. One of them explained that if she won the debate, "many men would have resented it. They would have said, 'There's my wife' and it wouldn't have been a good thing."[46] But far more often, the campaign highlighted Thatcher's housewifely identity. A series of photo opportunities at grocery stores allowed her to pose as an ordinary housewife who promised to run the country just as she ran the household: voters, she insisted, "will turn to me because they believe a woman *knows* about prices."[47] When interviewers questioned whether a woman could withstand the strain of running the country, Thatcher retorted, "Any woman who has had to get up at night to her children and still cope can stand this. By comparison, all this is a doddle."[48] (She never, of course, mentioned the nanny.)

On May 4, 1979, 76 percent of British voters went to the polls. Just under 44 percent of these voters cast their ballot for the Conservative Party, the lowest share won by the Conservatives since World War II. Nevertheless, because the British electoral system (like that of the United States) is based not on proportional representation but on the "winner takes all," the Conservatives won seventy more seats in the House of Commons than Labour. Significantly, over 5 percent of Conservative voters in 1979 had voted for Labour in the last election—the largest swing of voters from one party to another since 1945. Many of these former Labour voters came from the same section of British society that had produced Thatcher's parents and Thatcher herself: the upper working class and the lower middle class, skilled workers and small business owners.

As is traditional in the British political system, Thatcher moved immediately into Number 10 Downing Street, the prime minister's residence and seat of power in London. Standing on the front steps, she gave the usual short speech to the hordes of reporters before she entered the building. Her advisors had chosen the supposed prayer of St. Francis of Assisi (actually a nineteenth-century forgery) for her to quote:

> Where there is discord, may we bring harmony;
> Where there is error, may we bring truth;
> Where there is doubt; may we bring faith;
> And where there is despair, may we bring hope.

One Conservative politician described this choice of words as "the most awful humbug; it was so totally at odds with Margaret's belief in conviction politics and the need to abandon the consensus style of government."[49] Certainly, over the next decade, the first line came to seem increasingly ironic as Thatcher proved to be one of the most divisive political leaders in contemporary British history.

CHAPTER 5

| THE FALTERING START OF THE |
THATCHER REVOLUTION:
1979–1983

WHEN MARGARET THATCHER took office in 1979, she had one over-riding objective: to reverse her country's economic, interna-tional, and moral decline. "I can't bear Britain in decline. I just can't," she told a BBC interviewer.[1] Yet Thatcher's efforts to trans-late monetarist theories into practical policies sent the British economy into a tailspin and provoked outbursts of urban rioting not seen in Britain since the 1920s. Thatcher became the most hated prime minister in modern history. Many within her own Cabinet regarded both her and her politics with loathing. As a result, her first government was almost her last. Even within this first tumultuous term, however, Thatcher pushed ahead in oblit-erating the social democratic consensus by redefining Britain's global role, reshaping the British economy, and reversing the wel-fare state. The Thatcher Revolution was underway.

In many ways the Thatcher Revolution began in the Cabinet Room of 10 Downing Street. The British prime minister is not the equivalent of an American president. The "prime" in "prime min-ister" comes from the Latin "primus," or "first"; the prime minis-ter is supposed to be the first among equals. Over the course of

Thatcher's many years in office, however, Thatcher reshaped the British system so that it more closely resembled—not in structure but in actual power relations—the American presidential model. One way she did so was to limit her Cabinet's ability to shape policy. A number of factors contributed to this shift, including Thatcher's self-identity as a revolutionary, her personality and history, and above all, her suspicion of consensus politics.

Looking back on her time as prime minister just a few years after she left office, Thatcher described herself as "a Conservative

THE SUN CARTOON: SNOW WHITE AND THE DWARVES. *Although from 1975, and therefore several years before Thatcher formed her first government, this cartoon captures well Thatcher's leadership style: she rejected the "first among equals" tradition of Cabinet government and instead opted for a much more presidential role.*

revolutionary."[2] It was an accurate description. Like many revolutionaries, Thatcher's total commitment to her cause could sometimes seem fanatical and often made life difficult for those who had to work alongside her every day. Imbued with a sense of mission, she had little interest in exploring alternative ideas or points of view. As she put it, "Personally I was conscious that in some strange way I was instinctively speaking and feeling in harmony with the great majority of the population. Such moments are as unforgettable as they are rare. They must be seized to change history."[3]

Thatcher's conviction and certainty translated at times into a demand for total control, a demand strengthened by her personality. For example, her grasp of detail and her workaholism—one observer described her addiction to work as "maniacal"[4]—did not always translate into an effective prime-ministerial style. She had difficulty delegating. In a Cabinet government, each minister is supposed to be in charge of his or her department—his or her own "patch." Thatcher, however, could not resist trespassing on her colleagues' patches. Astonishingly energetic herself and able to get by day after day on just a few hours of sleep, she regarded the need for rest or time off as a sign of weakness.

Thatcher's insecurities also played a role here. She had grown up outside the circles of privilege and power and she never completely fit in with Britain's traditional upper class. Lacking the easy assumption of authority that still distinguished the British elite, she opted for aggression. Unfailingly polite and kind to servants, staffers, and backbencher MPs who were in no position to question her, Thatcher was often not just brusque but brutal to her political colleagues and advisors, many of whom were older, more politically experienced, and from a higher social class.

Thatcher's contempt for the politics of consensus was, however, the most important factor in shaping her leadership style. The Conservative MPs who made up her Cabinet quickly discovered that Thatcher had no patience for forming a group consensus, that she regarded compromise as morally weak, and that she loved to argue but hated to lose. Like many revolutionaries, she was convinced that she faced the threat of counterrevolution all around her, and she was not entirely wrong. Practical politics dictated that Thatcher include in her first Cabinet many Conservative stalwarts who were not in any way Thatcherites. She called these colleagues "wets"—a term borrowed from British boarding school slang that meant "weak, sentimental, soppy"—and was often openly contemptuous of them and their social democratic political views.

Suspicious of most of her colleagues, then, Thatcher usually came into Cabinet meetings with her mind already made up so that the sessions were devoted to the prime minister telling her Cabinet members what would and should be done. One aide estimated that at the weekly meetings, Thatcher talked for approximately 90 percent of the time.[5] The nickname "Attila the Hen" summed up Thatcher's scorched earth, take-no-prisoners approach to government. It did not endear her to her colleagues, but it shifted power from the Cabinet to the prime minister.

The Attila the Hen moniker is also, of course, deeply gendered. No man could or would be called a hen, and the parallel male terms—rooster, cock—carry rather different connotations. Hens peck; the imagery here was of the British Cabinet as a kind of hen-pecked collectivity, with Thatcher remorselessly, relentlessly jabbing away. Yet in British English, "hen" also has other connotations. "Hen party" is the common term for what in the United States is sometimes called a bachelorette party—a soon-to-be bride's night out with female friends and usually associated with a great deal of off-color behavior. There was not much of a hen party atmosphere in Thatcher's Cabinet (Thatcher appointed only one woman to a Cabinet-level position and then only for a brief time) but a kind of covert sexuality was never far away. Conservative MP Alan Clark wrote of her visit to the Commons cafeteria in 1980, "Goodness she is *so* beautiful, made-up to the nines . . . but still quite bewitching."[6] If a male—usually older—colleague found it difficult to argue forcefully against Thatcher because such behavior was not gentlemanly, she did not hesitate to press her advantage, nor did she fail to flirt when it served her purpose. Recognizing that the media would always subject her clothes and hair to far greater scrutiny that any man's, she paid careful attention to her appearance, often changing several times a day. She used clothes to project a feminine yet authoritative image. Her crisply detailed, never mannish, often vibrantly colored skirted suits highlighted the contrast between Thatcher and the interchangeable men in identical black suits who made up her Cabinet, and thus reinforced her image as a new sort of leader, with new policies and unshakeable principles.

One of those principles was that inflation threatened the very soul of the capitalist system. Thatcher regarded the battle against inflation as a key fight in her war against social democracy. Previous governments had erred, Thatcher believed, in trying to limit inflation by setting wages. Such an approach granted trade unions far too much political power and, more fundamentally, reflected the corporatist assumptions of a social democratic society. The only way to reduce inflation, she believed, was by following monetarist dictates: limit the money supply. But controlling the money supply meant far more than not printing pound notes. Government borrowing also increased the amount of money in circulation—and a key factor in ratcheting up government borrowing was maintaining the welfare state. To control inflation through monetarist policies, therefore, was to send a deadly arrow straight into the social democratic heart of the postwar settlement. It meant stripping trade unions of their political power; it meant reducing the size and cost of government and thus limiting its ability to intervene in economic life; it meant limiting government borrowing and thus reversing the growth of the welfare state; it meant replacing the communalist values of modern British society with an individualist ethos. For Thatcher, then, the battle against inflation was not just about curbing prices. As she put it, "Economics is the method. The object is to change the soul."[7]

The monetarist mantra of controlling the money supply also appealed to Thatcher's categorical mindset. She liked simplicities and certainties; she liked to divide the world into camps with clear boundaries—us versus them, capitalists and socialists, the savers and the spenders. But the simplicities and certainties of monetarist theory proved rather more nebulous and a great deal more complex when translated into actual policy. Thatcher approached monetary policy with confidence: money was something you could count. But *money*, in the globalized economy, is an abstract concept of such fluidity that counting and then controlling the actual money supply in a single country at a single point of time is like trying to mold mercury or to build a house out of water. How does a government define the money supply? Is it the money—notes and coins—in circulation, plus the assets held in things like checking accounts that can be easily converted into notes and coins? Or does it include less liquid assets such as certificates of deposit and debt securities that circulate very little? Which of these definitions provides the most efficient means of combatting inflation? During the first several months of Thatcher's first term in office, the monetary supply seemed a constantly shifting target that again and again the government failed to hit. Cabinet member Ian Gilmour protested that monetarism translated into the "uncontrollable in pursuit of the indefinable."[8] Meanwhile, inflation continued to climb. By the end of Thatcher's first year in office, the inflation rate had doubled from 10 to a shocking 22 percent.

The government's failure to meet or even clearly define its own monetary targets resulted in a rapid, but covert, retreat from monetarism. With the Budget of 1981 and all subsequent budgets during her time as prime minister, Thatcher returned to conventional Keynesian macroeconomic management tools and policies. In other words, Thatcher, like Heath, executed a U-turn from policies she had declared fundamental. Yet, unlike Heath, Thatcher's U-turn was barely noticed, then or since. She never admitted to it; she and Geoffrey Howe, her first Chancellor of the

Exchequer (the Cabinet minister in charge of economic and financial matters), continued to use the mysteries of monetarism to cloud and cover what they were actually doing. And what they were actually doing was turning Keynesian economics inside out: using the various fiscal tools at their disposal not to combat unemployment and encourage economic growth but rather to deflate the British economy. It eventually worked. By the middle of 1983, inflation was down to 4.5 percent. Hence, Thatcher "achieved the desired ends, albeit not by the promised means."[9]

The means, however, were brutal, and the desirability of the ends continues to be much debated. Faced with galloping inflation figures, Thatcher and Howe raised interest rates and then raised them again, to an astonishing 20 percent. These rates sucked investment out of industry and—even more devastating from the perspective of British manufacturers—helped keep the exchange rate of the pound high. A strong pound pleased stockbrokers, bankers, and financiers in the City (London's equivalent of Wall Street) and also pleased Thatcher, who regarded the strength of the national currency as a barometer of national power, but because British manufactured goods were now overpriced on export markets, it dealt an enormous blow to already struggling factories and firms. In effect, Thatcher presided over a De-Industrial Revolution in these years, a development made clear when, in 1983, for the first time since the early nineteenth century, Britain imported more manufactured goods than it exported. For British industry, the early 1980s were worse than the Great Slump of the 1920s and 1930s; overall, British manufacturing lost 25 percent of its capacity under Thatcher. She often spoke about the importance of small businesses to the British economy, but during every one of her years in office, small business bankruptcies outnumbered start-ups.

Thatcher argued then and her supporters argue now that these years marked a painful but necessary transition from Britain's old manufacturing economy to a new postindustrial economy based not on the making of things but on the delivery of services and information. Critics then and critics now counter that Thatcher's policies deepened the British recession unnecessarily, slashed manufacturing needlessly, and delayed economic recovery. What cannot be debated is the fact that as business after business shut down, unemployment rates pushed up and up and up. By the end of 1980, 2 million British men and women were unemployed—a level of joblessness not seen in Britain in over forty years. And the numbers just kept climbing. By the start of 1982, they hit 3 million, or a national unemployment average of 12.5 percent. Britain had one of the highest rates of unemployment in Europe, second only to Belgium. The traditional industrial heartlands—England's North and West Midlands, as well as much of Scotland, Wales, and Northern Ireland—saw unemployment rates of 20 percent. The devastation of mass unemployment had returned to the United Kingdom for the first time since the Great Depression.

Thatcher's taxation policies worsened the situation, at least in the short term. In keeping with the classical liberal belief that progressive income tax rates punished individuals for hard work and innovation, Thatcher supported her Chancellor of the Exchequer Geoffrey Howe in his decision to cut the highest rate of income tax from 84 to 60 percent, despite the inflationary results. To make up for the loss of government revenue, Howe doubled the VAT (Value Added Tax—a tax on consumption similar to a sales tax). This highly regressive tax policy not only strained family budgets in many homes, it also dampened demand for manufactured goods and so led to yet more business closures and job losses during Thatcher's first term.

With unemployment rates so high, many of Thatcher's advisors and Cabinet members argued that British society could not withstand such pressure and urged her to change course. Thatcher, however, refused to be diverted, as she made clear in a speech to the Conservative Party conference in October, 1980. Playing on the title of a well-known play (Christopher Fry's *The Lady's Not for Burning*) she declared, "To those waiting with bated breath for that favourite media catchphrase, the 'U' turn, I have only one thing to say. You turn if you want to. The lady's not for turning."[10]

Thatcher refused to turn, but British cities began to burn. In the spring of 1981, riots exploded in Brixton, a poor inner-city area in southern London. Protesters rampaged through London streets, lighting cars on fire, breaking shop windows, and pelting the police with rocks and Molotov cocktails. In July, the violence spread not only to other parts of London but also to Birmingham, Manchester, Liverpool, and numerous other cities. British society encountered its worst outbreak of civil unrest since 1919. Thatcher insisted that the riots arose not as a response to her policies but rather as a result of the permissive social legislation of the 1960s. "Society must have rules if it is to continue to be civilized," she declared.[11] She responded to the riots not by rethinking her policies but by equipping the police with water cannons, tear gas, rubber bullets, riot shields, body armor, and surveillance helicopters.

Thatcher's first term in office was thus a tumultuous time. Despite almost overwhelming economic disarray, social unrest, and political pressure, Thatcher pressed ahead with key aspects of her program. She did not revolutionize British society during her first government, but she did succeed in laying the groundwork for that revolution in three main areas: limiting trade union power, weakening the welfare state, and reducing the State's role in the economy.

As we saw in Chapter 4, the Winter of Discontent that preceded Thatcher's election led many Britons to view the unions as dangerous. To strip the unions of their ability to disrupt the British economy, Thatcher followed the policy that the Conservative Shadow Cabinet had crafted during its years in opposition in the later 1970s. The title of a key strategy paper, "Stepping Stones," epitomized this approach. To cross the river to union reform, the Conservative government would move stone by stone, step by step—or, to change the metaphor, rather than a head-on, all-out fight against the unions (such as Heath had tried—and lost), Conservatives committed themselves to a war of attrition. Thatcher's opening offensive, the Employment Act of 1980, was therefore limited in scope: while it weakened the unions' ability to impose a "closed shop" on a workplace (to require that all workers be union members), it did not ban closed shops. Similarly, it did not outlaw sympathy strikes (strikes to support other workers on strike), although it did restrict picketing to a worker's place of employment.

Far more important than what Thatcher did vis-à-vis the unions in her first government was what she did *not* do. Unlike all previous post–World War II prime ministers, she did not call union leaders into 10 Downing Street for consultation or negotiation. She simply ignored them—and so wrecked the basic mechanism of corporatism. And even more important, she allowed unemployment rates to climb. Mass unemployment proved far more effective than any legislation in slashing union power. In 1982, lengthy strikes by railway workers and by National Health Service (NHS) nurses ended in demoralizing union defeats. Thatcher's attitude was clear: "If you want more unemployment and more job losses, then keep on striking. Don't blame me."[12]

Like the unions, the welfare state was also a key target of Thatcherist reform. In a lecture in 1980, Thatcher explicitly rejected the "cradle to grave" social welfare promise of the postwar consensus: "We should not expect the State to appear in the guise of an extravagant good fairy at every christening, a loquacious and tedious companion at every stage of life's journey, the unknown mourner at every funeral."[13] Hence, despite the fact that record-breaking numbers of people were out of work, Thatcher's government cut unemployment benefits—and then taxed this reduced amount. Thatcher herself remained convinced that many of the unemployed chose not to work. To "tackle this problem of people better off out of work," she told one of her Cabinet members, "I think we will have to go back to soup kitchens."[14] Her initial budgets also imposed a series of spending reductions on other aspects of social security (which in the British system covers a huge and varied set of social services, including not only unemployment payments but also child allowances, sickness and disability benefits, and old-age pensions).

Yet, as with trade union reform, Thatcher did not mount an all-out offensive against the welfare state. An astute politician, she recognized that many of its elements, particularly the NHS, were genuinely popular and that middle-class Britons—"our people"—actually drew proportionately more benefits from the welfare state than did members of the working class. Thatcher thus moved cautiously in the realm of welfare reform. For example, rather than eliminate the universal, state-provided old-age pension, a step that would have aroused enormous protest, she instead cut the link between the value of the pension payment and the cost of living. This universal pension would thus wither on the vine: as inflation eroded its value year by year, people would learn not to rely on it or to regard it as an essential right, and those who could afford to would turn instead to private pensions.

As careful as Thatcher had to be in modifying Britain's social security provisions, she had to step even more cautiously into the dangerous terrain of health care reform. From the Thatcherist perspective, the NHS in many ways epitomized postwar socialism: With its "free at the point of delivery" ethos, it seemed to serve up something for nothing, to lead people to believe they could get what they needed or wanted without having to pay for it. In her very first speech as prime minister in the House of Commons, then, Thatcher warned, "There is no such thing as a free service in the Health Service."[15] Yet the NHS remained immensely popular and voters disliked any talk of tinkering with what had long been acclaimed as one of Britain's proudest postwar achievements. Thatcher received a sharp reminder of these facts in 1982, when the Cabinet discussed a Conservative think-tank proposal to implement radical cuts in the welfare state, including dismantling the NHS.[16] The Cabinet deliberations were leaked to the press and the ensuing uproar forced Thatcher to retreat quickly from the proposal and to insist, "The National Health Service is safe with us."[17]

While Thatcher could not, then, dismantle the NHS, she did endeavor to gut the social democratic political culture that regarded the health service as the equal possession of all. She encouraged the spread of private health insurance companies and told Cabinet ministers they should be ashamed to use the NHS when they could afford to pay for their own and their family's medical needs. Unlike previous prime ministers and political leaders who were proud to use the NHS, proud to show their commitment to and participation in this communal resource, Thatcher boasted of her private health care. She hoped to change the public attitude toward the NHS and she had some success, judging by the fact that private health insurance doubled during her years in office.

Just as Thatcher hoped to limit the state's responsibility in welfare, so she sought to reduce the state's involvement in industrial ownership and management. One of Thatcher's first actions as prime minister, then, was to freeze civil service recruitment and pay raises, and to establish an Efficiency Unit charged with looking for ways to economize in every government department. Such reductions, however, were simply the means to the far broader end of diminishing the presence of the state in British social and economic life. When Thatcher took office in 1979, the state directly owned 40 percent of Britain's economic output and indirectly controlled even more: "It ran railways, shipbuilding, car making, coal mining, ports and harbours, airlines and airports, gas, electricity, nuclear energy and arms manufacture. It owned the nation's hospitals, schools, prisons and old people's homes, and ran a national pension scheme."[18] Thatcher did not embark on wholesale privatization in her first term in office, but she did begin to make moves in that direction. The train system remained nationalized, for example, but British Rail hotels were sold off to private investors and private long-distance bus services were encouraged to compete with British Rail. The British National

Oil Corporation, set up in 1976 to compete with private firms in the production of North Sea oil, was partially privatized in 1982. Meanwhile, various state-owned industries were divided, in preparation for sales down the road.

In housing, however, Thatcher did not wait to implement dramatic privatization policies. As one of her deputies put it, "Housing was the area where Margaret Thatcher thought it was easiest to start to dismantle the dependency culture."[19] In 1979, public rented housing ("council houses") made up over 30 percent of all housing in the United Kingdom. By giving council housing tenants the right to buy their homes at subsidized rates, Thatcher aimed to build a "property-owning democracy," a society of independent property owners who would take care of themselves, their families, and their own property, rather than, as she saw it, relying on the state to care for them. The Housing Act of 1980 sought to realize this aim by requiring local governments to sell off council houses to willing tenants at a substantial discount. Over the next three years, 500,000 houses moved from the public to the private sector.

The "right-to-buy" housing legislation exemplified Thatcherism in many ways. It was extremely popular with those new homeowners who were able to take advantage of it and who often became enthusiastic Thatcher supporters and Conservative voters. Thatcher's insistence on extending mortgage-interest tax relief for homeowners (against the advice of members of her government) as a reward for "our people" further consolidated her hold on this voting bloc. But at the same time, the Housing Act significantly widened the gap between rich and poor in Britain. The most prosperous tenants bought the best houses; sharp cuts in rental subsidies for the tenants who remained—often in substandard housing—sometimes translated into almost a 100 percent rise in rents. The Housing Act also forbade local housing authorities from using the money from sales of council houses to construct any more public housing. With fewer affordable houses available for rent in a time of escalating unemployment, and with rents on those few houses rising rapidly, homelessness began to climb as well.

The advent of the property-owning democracy thus coincided with the return of homelessness as a major social problem. Thatcher had promised order and stability, but the sight of homeless beggars on their city streets led many Britons in the early 1980s to wonder whether Thatcherist individualism was actually tearing apart the social order. Divisions over race and immigration, Northern Ireland, and defense added to this sense of social disintegration during Thatcher's first government.

The British population remained overwhelmingly white in 1981, but in the cities especially, a new multicolored and multicultural Britain was taking shape—and many white Britons, including Thatcher, found this new shape uncomfortable. In 1979, for example, the new prime minister met with her advisors to discuss the possibility of offering sanctuary to refugees fleeing the communist regime in Vietnam. Thatcher opposed the move on the ground that it was "quite wrong" to give any Vietnamese housing preference over "white citizens"; however, she added that she "had less objections to refugees such as [white] Rhodesians, Poles and Hungarians since they could more easily be assimilated into British society."[20]

Although the riots of 1981 should not be oversimplified as race riots, race certainly played a role in the violence, particularly in Brixton. In this South London district, one-third of the housing was listed as substandard and residents, largely of Afro-Caribbean descent, had long complained of the aggressive policing tactics of the almost entirely white London Metropolitan Police Force. Moreover, people of color were particularly hard-hit by the recession under Thatcher's first government. While unemployment overall rose by two-thirds between 1980 and 1981, it spiked up by 82 percent among British blacks.

Thatcher's resolute stance against further New Commonwealth (i.e., non-white) immigration did little to calm racial tensions. The Nationality Act of 1981 demolished once and for all the principle established in 1948 that all Commonwealth citizens were entitled to citizenship and a related right of abode in the United Kingdom—or, as Conservative Cabinet member William Whitelaw put it, the new law dismissed "the lingering notion that Britain is somehow a haven for all those whose countries we used to rule."[21] At the same time, however, the act granted most Commonwealth citizens of (white) British descent the lifetime right to migrate to the UK. It thus reinforced rather than challenged another lingering notion, that to be British was to be white.

The question of Britishness also wove its way through one of the most divisive issues of Thatcher's first government: her hard line in Northern Ireland. By 1979, the "Troubles" had been raging for a decade, with terrorist outrages regularly punctuating not only life in the province but also in mainland Britain. The first years of the Troubles were the bloodiest: 200 British soldiers and 600 civilians (including paramilitaries) died between 1971 and 1973. Through the rest of the 1970s, annual British military deaths in Northern Ireland averaged about twelve per year. A few months after Thatcher took office, an IRA bomb assassinated Lord Mountbatten (the last Viceroy of India and Prince Charles' godfather) and two of his family members; that same day eighteen British soldiers were slaughtered in an IRA ambush—the single largest military loss that the British military endured during the lengthy campaign in Northern Ireland.

Then, in 1981, one of the most famous hunger strikes in modern Western history presented Thatcher with an even greater challenge. In March, Bobby Sands, the highest ranking IRA leader in the Maze prison in Northern Ireland, declared his determination to go on a hunger strike until IRA prisoners were granted political rather than criminal status. Two weeks after Sands began his fast, a second prisoner joined Sands in refusing food; two weeks after that, a third; and on until twenty-three men were on hunger strike. To Thatcher, these men were convicted murderers and nothing more. "Murder is murder is murder," Thatcher insisted. "It is not now and never can be a political crime. So there is no question of political status."[22] She refused to budge, even after Northern Irish voters in the district of Fermanagh and South Tyrone elected Sands (still on hunger strike, still in prison) to the British Parliament. Sands died on May 5, 1981, followed by nine more hunger strikers over the next several weeks—and seventy-three people who were killed in the street violence stirred up by these events. Finally, after representatives of the Roman Catholic Church convinced the families of the men still alive to intervene, the IRA called off the strike.

Thatcher won. Her willingness to let the hunger strikers kill themselves made clear to the world her iron resolution—many would say her ruthlessness. Yet her victory in this case was Pyrrhic. The sight of men willing to starve themselves to death for the sake of a cause moved observers around the world and won for the IRA tremendous sympathy, while Thatcher herself was often vilified as a murderer. In the United States, especially, press coverage tended to paint Sands and the other nine men as martyrs and to depict Britain as a colonialist occupier. American contributions poured into IRA pockets and ensured the continuation of the Troubles over the next decade.

Thatcher's strong stance in Northern Ireland mirrored her approach to foreign policy. Convinced that the professional diplomats in the Foreign Office were far too conciliatory and concerned about international opinion rather than British interests, she was determined from the very start of her premiership to assume a more aggressive stance. Such an aim was in many ways audacious. Thatcher had no experience in foreign affairs. She spoke no foreign languages and before she became Conservative Party leader had rarely traveled abroad. Yet she moved quickly to reassert a leading role for Britain in the world.

Thatcher viewed foreign policy in the same binary, Us-versus-Them terms in which she saw Britain: *We* had to stand firm, eschew compromise, and defeat *Them*. The identity of *Them* was never in doubt. In Thatcher's view, the Soviet Union posed a clear and present danger to the peace and prosperity of the Western world. An ardent cold warrior, she was convinced that the years of détente had allowed the Soviet Union not only to leap ahead in military power at the expense of NATO and the West but also to expand communist influence into Africa and Latin America. "Conviction politics" demanded a strong stance and a refusal to compromise.

Despite her overall aim of reducing government spending, therefore, Thatcher committed to increasing Britain's contributions to NATO by 3 percent. She also reaffirmed her belief in Britain's "independent nuclear deterrent" (in reality a nuclear defense system dependent on American technology and military power). This commitment meant that at a time of budgetary crisis, Thatcher pushed ahead with the expensive purchase of Trident nuclear submarines from the United States and the deployment of 160 American-owned ground-launched cruise nuclear missiles at bases in the United Kingdom. Her government also updated *Protect and Survive*; this civil defense manual, first published in the late 1950s, outlined in cheerful terms what an ordinary family should do if nuclear bombs landed on Britain. In the context of the early 1980s, its more cynical readers tended to regard the advice as a form of black comedy.

Thatcher's revving up of the cold war was intertwined with her passionate pro-Americanism. Convinced that Britain's strength rested on the Atlantic alliance, she placed the cultivation of a good relationship with the United States at the heart of her foreign policy. Fortunately for Thatcher, her rejection of détente and her hardline cold war stance paralleled a corresponding shift in American foreign policy. She came into office the same year that the Soviet invasion of Afghanistan prompted US President Jimmy Carter to back off from détente and call for economic and cultural sanctions against the Soviet Union, including a Western boycott of the Olympic Games in Moscow. Thatcher supported Carter and was furious that British athletes—and European leaders—refused to do the same.

Thatcher, however, was not particularly impressed with Carter overall. She thought he had "an unsure handle on economics" and "no large vision of America's future."[23] She had no such reservations about Ronald Reagan, who succeeded Carter in 1981. With Reagan, Thatcher recalled, "I knew that I was talking to someone who instinctively felt and thought as I did."[24] He was her genuine ideological partner, someone who shared not only her antagonism toward détente but also her equation of Soviet-style communism with Western social democracy and her belief that government was the problem, not the solution. The two leaders not only respected each other; they genuinely liked each other, despite (or perhaps because of) the contrast between Reagan's easy-going governing style and Thatcher's detail-oriented, obsessive workaholism. She had no reservations about being, in her words, "his principal cheerleader in NATO."[25] Cheerleaders, however, rarely formulate game strategy and bark plays from the sidelines. Thatcher's personality suited her far more for the role of head coach. According to Richard Perle (who served as assistant secretary of defense in Reagan's administration), "She never approached the conversations she had . . . with American officials and with the President from a position of supplication or inferiority. Quite the contrary."[26]

Thatcher's defense policies and her pro-Americanism, like so much else during her first term, divided the British people. Many Britons cheered her assertiveness and were relieved to see Britain resuming what they saw as its rightful place. Others resented the increased military expenditures at a time when the jobless saw their unemployment benefits cut. Still others decried her close relationship with Reagan and warned that the new hard line toward the Soviet Union would encourage rather than deter nuclear conflict. By April 1980, 40 percent of those polled believed that nuclear war would break out within ten years. The Campaign for Nuclear Disarmament (CND), first formed in 1958, experienced a massive resurgence, and, in 1981, a small group of women

CHAMPIONS OF THE NEW CONSERVATISM I. *By the time this photograph was taken in 1981, Thatcher and Reagan had developed a close working relationship.*

camped outside Greenham Common RAF base, the start of almost twenty years of a continuous on-site women's antinuclear protest. Thatcher, however, dismissed these protests as non-sensical. She believed that nuclear weapons had kept the peace for almost forty years and would continue to do so. "We are the true peace movement," she insisted.[27]

"Peace," however, was not a word that many observers associated with Thatcher in the early 1980s. She estranged many of her party colleagues with her brusque governing style; most of her own Cabinet believed deflationary fiscal policies were ruining the British economy and must be abandoned; the summer riots revealed serious tensions in British society; the IRA hunger strikes alienated much of global opinion; and the world seemed to be edging closer to nuclear war. Thatcher's ratings were the lowest of any prime minister since opinion polling began.

Thatcher's political position at this time was made even more precarious by the astounding rise of a new force in British politics, the Social Democratic Party (SDP). The SDP arose from a split in the Labour Party. Like Thatcher, many Labour supporters had responded to the economic crisis of the 1970s by concluding that the time had come to abandon the postwar social democratic consensus. Unlike Thatcher, however, they argued that the solution to Britain's economic and social woes lay in socialism. As Labour moved sharply to the left, with calls for the unilateral nuclear disarmament of Britain, the expansion of the nationalized sector of the economy, and the abolition of the House of Lords, Labour moderates found themselves marginalized. In 1981, four of the most prominent of these moderates declared that they were leaving Labour to form a new party, one that would be faithful to the social democratic principles on which they believed the traditional labor movement rested. In alliance with the small but long-established British Liberal Party, the new SDP suddenly seemed a major force in British politics. Voters who were distressed by Thatcherism but horrified by Labour's leftism flocked to the new alternative. In opinion polls in early 1982, the SDP was the most popular political party in Britain, with over 50 percent support.

With SDP candidates winning what had been seen as safe Conservative seats in two by-elections (known in the United

States as special elections—called in the middle of a term because of an MP's death or disqualification), Thatcher seemed to be leading her party to sure defeat. Thatcherism appeared to be a short-lived, disastrous experiment. Journalists and MPs were placing bets not on if, but when, Thatcher would fall. And then on April 2, 1982, Argentine forces invaded the Falklands Islands. The resulting war saved Thatcher and allowed the success of Thatcherism. Military victory not only rescued her government; it also catapulted her into such a secure position as party leader that she was able to push through the Thatcherist agenda and remake Britain along Thatcherist lines. As Thatcher's predecessor as prime minister put it, "I wish I had had a war."[28]

A small archipelago in the south Atlantic, the Falklands were home to 1,800 people, 650,000 sheep, and 10 million penguins. The islands lay just 250 miles from the coast of Argentina but 8,000 miles from Britain. Once useful to the navy as a refueling station, they had long ceased to have any real strategic or economic value for Britain. Nevertheless, British governments had refused to acquiesce to Argentine claims on the islands because the islanders saw themselves as British. Ironically, Thatcher's Nationality Act of 1981 actually removed British citizenship from the Falkland Islanders; nevertheless, Thatcher regarded the Falklanders as "British in stock and tradition" and she went to war to defend that Britishness.[29]

Even more ironically, the Falklands War cemented Thatcher's reputation as a strong leader and even a warrior, although the war itself was a result of significant weaknesses in her defense policy. Despite clear intelligence showing that the Argentine government was contemplating a forcible seizure of the Falklands, Thatcher approved the decision to withdraw the HMS *Endurance*, the sole British patrol ship left in the South Atlantic—part of a range of massive cuts to the navy. These cuts, combined with the new denial of British citizenship to the Falkland Islanders, were mistakenly viewed by the Argentines as signals that Britain would not contest their occupation of the islands.

British victory in the Falklands was by no means guaranteed. A seaborne attack, without air cover, against an enemy well entrenched on land was the stuff of military nightmares. Fortunately for Thatcher, the British troops fought with a degree of professionalism and killing efficiency that won them respect around the world, and the poorly trained Argentines gave way quickly. By all accounts, Thatcher proved herself a superb wartime leader (although, of course, the war only lasted a few months). She did not interfere in military decisions, she stayed resolutely within the boundaries of international and military law, and she gave the soldiers her full support. In private, she found the war both exhausting and terrifying; she wrote a personal letter to the family of every serviceman killed and at times broke down in tears, but in public she expressed absolute confidence that Britain would win.

Britain did win, but it was an expensive victory. Almost 1,000 soldiers died (one for every two islanders). The dead included 255 British servicemen; another 777 were wounded (including about 70 permanently disabled). The casualty count continued to grow in the years after the war ended, with more Falklands veterans taking their own lives than died in combat. The financial cost of the expedition and of securing the Falklands afterward ran to £3 billion—a huge sum for a nation in the midst of severe recession. In the wake of the victory, moreover, Thatcher canceled the planned naval cuts. As John Campbell has put it, "By recovering the Falklands the navy saved itself."[30]

For Thatcher, the gains far outweighed the losses. She had set out to reverse British international decline and here was Britain, once again sailing the seas and putting the world to rights. From the Falklands War on, British prime ministers once again viewed overseas interventions as part and parcel of Britain's role in the world, as later events in Iraq and Afghanistan would demonstrate. The British public overwhelmingly supported the war. After all, British "kith and kin" had been attacked and British soil had been invaded. Moreover, it seemed such a comfortably old-fashioned war—no nuclear weapons and no terrorists, instead the almost nostalgic sight of British sailors leaning over the sides of ships and waving good-bye to their women on shore, the British navy sailing the seas in defense of the vulnerable, the Union Jack flying confidently. After decades of decline, of the relentless rhythm of currency crises and budget deficits and industrial strife, this reassertion of British power *felt good*. Thatcher made the most of this upswing in national sentiment. "We have ceased to be a nation in retreat . . . Britain has re-kindled that spirit which has fired her for generations past and which today has begun to burn as brightly as before. Britain found herself again in the South Atlantic," she declared.[31]

During and after the war, Thatcher's popularity ratings soared upward. Many Conservative voters who had flirted with the SDP-Liberal Alliance rushed back to "our Maggie." Nevertheless, Thatcher remained a polarizing figure. In the general election of June 1983, the Conservative share of the popular vote actually fell somewhat from what it had been in 1979. The winner-take-all system, however, added fifty-eight seats in the House of Commons to the Conservative total and ensured Thatcher's position as party—and as national—leader.

CHAPTER 6

THATCHER'S TRIUMPH: 1984–1987

ON OCTOBER 12, 1984, the IRA almost killed Mrs. Thatcher. She was, as usual, up late working, completing last-minute revisions on the speech she was to give to the Conservative Party Conference in a few hours' time. Just before 3:00 a.m., a bomb exploded in the Brighton hotel where Thatcher and the Cabinet were staying. Although thrown back by the blast, the prime minister escaped unhurt. Many other hotel guests were not so lucky. Five people died and several more were left permanently injured. To the amazement and admiration of the world, Thatcher did not cancel the conference or her speech that morning. Instead, she walked into the conference hall precisely on schedule, stepped up to the podium, and declared, "The fact that we are gathered here now, shocked but composed and determined, is a sign not only that this attack has failed but that all attempts to destroy democracy by terrorism will fail."[1]

Thatcher's courageous performance in Brighton cemented the reputation for steely resolve that she had won during the Falklands War and made it clear to both her supporters and her opponents, both at home and abroad, that she deserved the title of Iron Lady. By the time of the Brighton bombing, Thatcher's second term in office was well underway and it was during this second term that Thatcherism triumphed. The transformation of the

British economy accelerated, while a series of radical reform measures dismantled key elements of the social democratic structures erected in Britain in the years after World War II. Thatcher herself was hailed as the leader of a global movement, of New Conservatism. Yet even during Thatcher's second triumphant term in office, the Thatcher Revolution encountered important limits. Thatcher herself remained an extremely divisive figure and many of the changes that she initiated led Britain in a direction rather different than what she had intended.

When British troops returned from the Falklands, they marched in an old-fashioned victory parade down the streets of central London. In a striking innovation, however, Margaret Thatcher rather than Queen Elizabeth stood on hand to receive the soldiers' salute. Thatcher's usurpation of the queen's traditional role signaled her new ascendancy not only in national but in global politics. Commentators noted how her foreign trips became ever more regal, with the prime minister stepping off planes to be greeted by military honor guards and little girls with flower bouquets. Thatcher herself increasingly used the royal we (most notoriously in 1989, when she announced, "We have become a grandmother"[2]).

The first British prime minister in over two decades to play a significant role on the world stage, Thatcher was by the mid-1980s universally recognized as the leader of a New Conservatism that reached beyond Britain's shores. When Ronald Reagan took the oath of office as US president in 1981, Thatcher welcomed him as a partner in her war against social democracy. One year later, a third important New Conservative took office: Helmut Kohl, leader of West Germany's Christian Democratic Party and chancellor of West Germany (and later a reunited Germany) from 1982 to 1998. Kohl was a somewhat uneasy member of the New Conservative triumvirate for both personal and political reasons. Unlike Reagan, he never developed a warm friendship, or even a cordial working relationship, with Thatcher. Moreover, as a Christian Democrat, Kohl retained a good bit of the Catholic paternalism

<small>Champions of the New Conservatism II. *Although they shared many of the same political convictions, Thatcher and German chancellor Helmut Kohl were often privately at odds. Thatcher's open antipathy toward the European Union made her unpopular with many continental politicians.*</small>

and concern for the communal good that shaped European Christian Democratic politics, and thus he proved more willing to allow the state an activist role than either Thatcher or Reagan.

Nevertheless, Kohl, too, preached the need for an economic and moral revolution—what he called *die Wende*, or the turning point, and he summed up this turning point in words familiar to and favored by both Thatcher and Reagan: "Less state, more market; fewer collective burdens, more personal performance; fewer encrusted structures, more mobility, self-initiative, and competition."[3] The elections of Reagan and Kohl thus confirmed and consolidated the New Conservative policies and principles that Thatcher had been proclaiming since she became Leader of the Conservative Party in 1975. As she put it in a speech to the party conference in 1986, "The policies the Government has pioneered are catching on in country after country."[4]

At the same time, changes in self-identified *leftist* governments also dramatically testified to the triumph of Thatcherism. By the early 1980s, continuing stagflation forced Socialist governments in Italy, Greece, and Spain to adopt Thatcherist policies: reduced health and social security expenditures, higher utility and public transport fees, and cuts in wages. France provides perhaps the best example of social democracy in retreat. Elected president in 1981, Socialist Party leader François Mitterrand promised his voters a series of radical social democratic measures, including a rise in the minimum wage, a reduction in the work week and an increase in vacation time, expanded social welfare, and nationalization of the banking system. But in 1982, a series of economic catastrophes—falling exports, rising trade and budget deficits, soaring inflation—forced Mitterand to cut social spending, reverse his nationalization program, implement austerity measures, and let unemployment rise. Throughout much of western Europe, then, social democracy seemed in retreat as Thatcherism advanced. Certainly Thatcher saw it that way. As she told the annual Conservative Party women's gathering, "Foreign countries may take their cuisine from Paris, but they take their economics from London."[5]

Thatcher's influence even extended across the Iron Curtain into the Soviet Union. Throughout her political career Thatcher had stood as an ardent cold warrior, always scathing in her view of Soviet communism and Western advocates of détente. But in 1984, Thatcher traveled to Moscow for the funeral of Soviet leader Yuri Andropov, where she met Mikhail Gorbachev, then the youngest member of the Soviet Politburo. She was instantly drawn to Gorbachev; she later recalled, "I spotted him because I was searching for someone like him."[6] Thatcher recognized that Gorbachev represented a new generation of Soviet leaders, someone open to new ways of thinking, someone, as she put it, that she could "do business with."[7] She invited him to London, and when he came at the end of the year, she admitted, "I found myself liking him." A few months later, yet another funeral catapulted

Mikhail Gorbachev into power. Suddenly and strangely, then, Thatcher, the anti-communist Iron Lady, had a warm working relationship with the leader of the Soviet Union. And she was right about Gorbachev. Although a committed communist, he acknowledged that the Soviet economy was broken; to fix it, he called for *perestroika,* or the restructuring of Soviet institutions, including the introduction of a limited market economy. In meetings and telephone conversations over the next several years, Thatcher encouraged Gorbachev's moves toward economic reform.

She also helped foster the growing relationship between Gorbachev and Reagan—a relationship that would be key in ending the cold war. Playing the role of mediator between the two, Thatcher helped persuade each of the genuineness of the other. Her opponents often derided her as "Reagan's poodle," but Thatcher lectured the American president just like she lectured members of her own Cabinet and was, according to Reagan administration member Richard Perle, "frequently the dominant influence in decision-making."[8] In one amazing week, she hosted Gorbachev in Britain, flew to China for a scheduled meeting, then headed to Washington, D.C. to meet with Reagan, and back to London—three continents and fifty-five hours of flying in five days, without any sign of jetlag. Vaulted into global prominence by the Falklands War and recognized as a leader in the New Conservative shift, Thatcher thus emerged during her second term in office as the most influential British leader in world affairs since Winston Churchill.

Her starring role on the world stage allowed Thatcher to color Britain's foreign policy in a New Conservative shade. Because she saw aid to developing nations as a kind of global welfare state—costly and counterproductive, sure to foster dependency rather than self-sufficiency—Britain's foreign aid budget declined during the 1980s. Access to the aid that remained was tied to trade deals that benefited British firms, frequently to the thriving British arms trade. Under Thatcher, Britain's rank as a global supplier of military equipment climbed from fifth to second in the world, trailing only the United States. Thatcher personally assisted in many arms deals, hammering out contracts with other world dealers and lobbying on behalf of UK firms (a number of which employed her son Mark as a well-paid consultant). Trade was trade, to Thatcher, and trade rather than aid led out of poverty, whether at home or abroad.

The other central pillar of Thatcher's foreign policy was maintaining the Atlantic alliance. Her much-vaunted "special relationship" with Reagan and Reagan's America did show strains at times, but Thatcher never wavered in her pro-Americanism or in her conviction that the most important perspective for Britain was the view across the Atlantic. In 1983, for example, Reagan failed to consult or even to inform Thatcher before American troops mounted an invasion of the Commonwealth nation of Grenada in an effort to restore political stability after a military coup. Although furious, Thatcher could do nothing. Moreover, three years later, when Reagan needed her support for a risky foreign adventure, Thatcher braved a domestic political firestorm to provide it. In 1986, the American president authorized the bombing of Libya in retaliation for the Libyan dictator Muammar Gaddafi's active support of terrorist groups. The Libya bombing met with widespread condemnation: the governments of France, Italy, and Spain all refused to allow American planes in their air space. In contrast, Thatcher permitted the Americans to use RAF bases for the strike force, despite the opposition of over 70 percent of the British public. She always recognized that the United States was clearly the senior partner in the special relationship, but she insisted that British and American interests ultimately coincided.

Thatcher's pro-Americanism contrasted sharply with her ambivalence, and often her open hostility, toward Europe and Britain's membership in the European Community (EC; today's EU). When Thatcher moved into 10 Downing Street in 1979, Britain had been a member of the EC for five years, yet both the

Conservative and the Labour parties, and the British electorate, remained sharply divided about whether or not this membership was a good thing. When the European Community first formed in 1956, the British government chose not to join, primarily to protect preferential trading relationships with other countries within the Empire and Commonwealth, but also because of the widely held conviction that Britain was a global, not just a European, power. As EC member states surged ahead of Britain in a number of key economic indices, however, many British policymakers regretted the decision to remain outside Europe. In the 1960s, both the Conservatives (in 1961, under Harold Macmillan) and Labour (in 1967, under Harold Wilson) applied to join the EC—and both experienced the humiliation of having the application vetoed by French leader Charles De Gaulle, who regarded postwar Britain as nothing more than an American puppet state.

Not until 1973, then (with De Gaulle now dead), did Britain "enter Europe." It did so under the Conservative government of Edward Heath. An enthusiastic European, Heath believed that membership in the EC was the solution to Britain's economic woes. He promised that joining the EC would "get us going again" and that this jumpstart offered Britain "the chance of new greatness."[9] Yet many members of the parliament, of the public, and even of Heath's own party disagreed. In the House of Commons on the day that MPs voted on EC entry, extraordinary scenes occurred, with members pushing, kicking, and swearing at each other.

The wider British public was also split on the issue. Businessmen, the national press, and the majority of public intellectuals favored Heath's European push, but as late as April 1971, at least 70 percent of the British public polled declared themselves opposed. Heath's government mounted a massive propaganda campaign to persuade voters of the benefits of entry, but most remained unenthusiastic. In the early 1970s, few of the British thought of themselves as European. As narrow as the English Channel is, it still marked a significant cultural barrier. Britain's

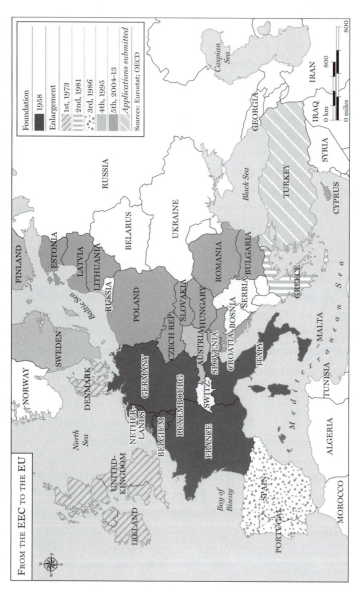

FROM THE EEC TO THE EU

Foundation
1958
Enlargement
1st, 1973
2nd, 1981
3rd, 1986
4th, 1995
5th, 2004-13
Applications submitted

Sources: Eurostat; OECD

MAP 2. FROM THE EUROPEAN ECONOMIC COMMUNITY TO THE EUROPEAN UNION

economic and military orientation had long been outward, to the Empire. Transforming an imperial identity into a European one would take time. Moreover, because many people could still remember World War II, hostility toward Germans persisted, while contempt for all things French remained deeply embedded in British culture. Practical matters also played a role. Throughout the 1950s and 1960s, for example, balance-of-payments crises meant that British families could bring only £50 per year outside the country; few, therefore, opted for continental holidays. Europe remained foreign.

Thatcher shared this instinctive anti-Europe outlook. In the last book she ever wrote, she contended, "During my lifetime most of the problems the world has faced have come . . . from mainland Europe."[10] In her view, *being British* was fundamentally different from and in many ways opposed to *being European*. In particular, Thatcher saw the interventionist state as a continental tradition against which British identity had been forged and British freedoms had been won. She also, at least at times, seemed to regard Europeans as deficient, inferior in key ways to the British, "our people." As education secretary in Heath's government, she even vetoed a plan for student exchanges with continental universities on the grounds that such a system would work to the benefit of foreigners but had nothing to offer British students.

Nevertheless, as a Conservative Cabinet member in 1973, Thatcher faithfully supported Heath in his decision to take Britain into Europe. Her support for EC membership, however, rested on two rather narrow bases: first, her belief that the EC served as the economic counterpart to NATO and hence a necessary demonstration of Western solidarity against the threat of the Soviet bloc, and second, her faith in free trade. In Thatcher's eyes, the EC was strictly an economic institution, a common (free) market meant to facilitate the buying and selling of goods and services. She rejected completely the vision of a politically united Europe that had motivated the original EC planners and that continued to inspire many Europeans.

Thatcher's deep-rooted mistrust of Continental Europeans and her economic definition of the EC structured her policies toward the Community once she became prime minister. She continued to support British membership in the Community for economic reasons, but she did little to rally her still-divided party on this issue, and she did even less to unite the nation behind its new European identity. Instead, by openly voicing her suspicions of Brussels and its bureaucrats, she exploited and thereby legitimized and strengthened popular anti-European prejudices.

She did so first by confronting the rest of the EC on an issue that appealed to most British voters: money, specifically the amount of money that Britain contributed annually to the Community. By the end of the 1970s, Britain contributed about £1 billion more to the EC than it received back from the EC in economic benefits. To most of the EC's leaders, Thatcher's insistence on evaluating EC membership on a purely cost-benefit basis entirely missed the point of the European Community. To Thatcher, however, the matter was simple. The EC had Britain's money (she soon began to call it "my money") and she wanted it back. She took an exceptionally hard line, refusing to consider any other EC matter until this budgetary dispute was settled, and dismissing any chances for settling the dispute within the context of other issues.

Thatcher's intractability did get results, with a partial refund won in 1980 and a further settlement in 1984, but it also widened the gap between Britain and the rest of Europe. It poisoned Thatcher's relations with her European colleagues and further tainted popular British perceptions of the EC. Thatcher's contempt for the usual diplomatic procedures infuriated other European leaders. The German chancellor Helmut Schmidt pretended to sleep during one meeting when Thatcher was speaking, the French premier Valery Giscard d'Estaing took to snubbing her publicly, and many Europeans bewailed the amount of time and effort spent on the "Bloody British Question." Thatcher responded in kind, dismissing most of her European colleagues as "a rotten lot."[11] The controversy played extremely well at home, where the tabloid press cheered Maggie and her victory over those bureaucrats in Brussels. By cementing a populist Us-versus-Them view of Europe, Thatcher guaranteed that the question of British membership in the EC would remain exactly that: a question, a matter of intense debate rather than a settled fact.

Thatcher's laser-like focus on the budget quarrel also meant that she did not pay much attention when, in 1983, the European Commission summit in Stuttgart produced what came to be known as the Stuttgart Declaration, asserting that the member states of the Community intended to move ahead toward greater unity on a broad range of issues, including foreign policy, defense, and human rights.[12] Despite her innate suspicion of Europeans, Thatcher had difficulty believing that any political leader, even a European, could actually envision the European Community as "an embryo United States of Europe."[13]

Her failure to grasp the power of such a vision led Thatcher, ironically, to play a leading role in the passage of the Single European Act of 1986. This act constituted an important step toward the creation of the European Union, with a parliament, a defense force, a single currency, and sweeping powers over member states. Thatcher, in other words, helped to make the "embryo United States of Europe" that she so abhorred a reality, although that is not what she intended to do. The Single European Act focused on what then-President of the European Commission Jacques Delors labeled *les quatres libertés* (the four freedoms): goods, services, capital, and people. To create a genuinely free common market, all four were to be released from undue regulation and restraint. An ardent free marketer, Thatcher embraced the Act, without seeming to comprehend—or at least refusing to acknowledge—that the legislation limited national sovereignty over economic matters. She could not see, perhaps because the vision was just so horrific to her, that other European leaders viewed the Act very differently, that they saw the economic common market as not an end but a means, a means to the end of political unification. Later, she argued that she had been duped and betrayed by her European counterparts: "I trusted them. I believed in them. I believed this was good faith between nations co-operating together. So we got our fingers burned." [14] But in 1986, she did not yet see it that way. She believed that, with the Single European Act, the EC was moving in a Thatcherist direction by shedding regulations and freeing up markets.

With the world seemingly falling in line behind her New Conservatism, Thatcher moved forward in her second term as prime minister to effect and consolidate the Thatcher Revolution at home. She encountered only limited success, however, in the area of social welfare rollback. Thatcher's secretary of state for social services carried out no fewer than four major reviews during his seven years in office in an effort to find ways to cut costs and increase efficiency. He never, however, reduced the level of social spending, largely because high levels of unemployment translated into high expenditures on unemployment benefits.

What Thatcher's second government did succeed in doing was to chip away at the principle of universality that had structured social welfare since the end of World War II. This principle rested not only on the ideal of social citizenship and the belief that all citizens had the right to a decent standard of living but also on pragmatism. In constructing and maintaining the welfare state, both Labour and Conservative governments had assumed that only if the wealthier, more educated, more powerful sectors of society shared in its benefits would they be willing to pay the taxes needed to ensure that its services were not second-rate. Thatcher, however, regarded the universal provision of welfare services as costly and morally dangerous. She wanted to focus social benefits on the "deserving poor," to push the undeserving to take responsibility for their own lives, and to encourage individuals with means to rely on the private rather than state sector.

The reform of old-age pensions during Thatcher's second government illustrated these aims. In her first government, Thatcher had severed the link between inflation and the basic state pension available to all. Most people with a steady employ-ment record, however, also had a second pension, either a private pension through their employer or a state-provided pension called SERPS (State Earned Related Pensions Scheme). Thatcher wanted to abolish SERPS but had to accept a compromise mea-sure. SERPS remained, but its value was cut (only half the pen-sion rather than the whole would now pass to widows, for example) and generous incentives encouraged individuals to opt for private plans instead.

Thatcher's attempts to mold the National Health Service (NHS) into a more Thatcherist shape were even less successful that her efforts to reform the welfare state. After her second elec-tion, Thatcher dared to move more directly to change the NHS. As popular as the service was, by the 1980s, the aging of the British population was straining the NHS's resources, and, as a result, the quality of British medical care was slipping in compar-ison to that provided in other western European countries. Britain, in fact, had long made do with less: while western European states spent approximately 10 percent of their GNP on their national health systems, the NHS consumed only 6 percent of the British GNP. Thatcher, however, believed the NHS's prob-lems were the result of mismanagement rather than underfund-ing. The NHS needed to be run more like a business—and so she turned to a successful businessman.

In 1983, Thatcher appointed Sir Roy Griffiths, who had run the very successful Sainsbury's supermarket chain, to review the health service. Griffiths declared himself appalled by what he found: "If Florence Nightingale were carrying her lamp through the corridors of the NHS today, she would almost certainly be searching for the people in charge."[15] Griffiths called for the cre-ation of a central management board and for the addition of pro-fessional management staffs to regional and district authorities. Sir Roy acknowledged that the addition of such staff—none of them actually treating patients—would of course add to the costs of the NHS, but he was confident that once these management professionals had applied their expertise to the health service, the resulting cost-cutting would more than pay off.

It did not work out that way. Costs climbed while the standard of care declined. Waiting lists for surgeries and treatments—many of them time critical—lengthened. Some district health authorities ran through their allotted budget before the end of the fiscal year and so could not treat their patients. The British press labeled the result the "postcode lottery" approach to health care: an individual's access to health care depended on the postcode (the British version of a zip code) in which he or she lived. Nurses went on strike, doctors threatened to do the same, and poll after poll showed that the British public did not trust Thatcher to care for what most people still regarded as a vital social resource and a proud national achievement.

The standard bearer of the Revolution during Thatcher's second government was not, then, the remaking of the NHS or welfare rollback but rather privatization (or denationalization). Even as a young Conservative candidate in the early 1950s, Thatcher had spoken out against the postwar Labour government's nationalization of key British industries, and throughout the 1950s and into the 1960s had made clear that her sympathies lay with the large numbers in the Conservative rank-and-file who demanded privatization. From the Thatcherist perspective, the nationalized industries represented all that was wrong with Britain and with the postwar consensus. As one Conservative MP put it, "Look, we're bloody fed up with them. They make huge losses, they have bolshie unions, and they are feather-bedded."[16] Private ownership in the competitive marketplace would, from this perspective, not only enhance industrial production and accelerate economic growth; it would also eliminate political bureaucracy, weaken trade union power, and diminish socialist ("bolshie" or Bolshevist) influence. And more immediately, selling off nationalized industries promised to inject huge amounts of revenue into the British Treasury.

During Thatcher's first government, her ministers experimented with limited privatization on a small scale, but in 1984, the full-bore privatization of the British economy began with the selling of shares in British Telecom. Much to Thatcher's delight, the stock sale proved an immense success and poured £3.9 billion into the government coffers. The success with British Telecom spurred on the privatization of British Gas, British Airways, the National Bus Company, and the Jaguar and British Leyland car companies. As each privatization measure was announced, opinion polls showed a majority of British citizens opposed; yet public enthusiasm for share buying quickly overcame this opposition. Many Britons joined the ranks of stockowners for the first time. Whereas only 3 million British citizens had owned stock in 1980, by 1990, 11 million did so. Thatcher hailed these numbers as evidence of a new enterprise economy.

The advent of the enterprise economy was not without significant problems. To encourage share sales, Thatcher's government deliberately set the initial share price below market levels; in other words, it undervalued what were essentially national assets. In addition, advertising campaigns and other processing costs ran into the billions. By one calculation, total government costs amounted to almost 18 percent of the proceeds of privatization and represented a net loss to British taxpayers.[17]

Moreover, although Thatcher prided herself on her good-housekeeper approach to economic matters, she allowed the Treasury to treat these one-time revenues as if they constituted stable sources of income. Rather than investing this money, the Treasury used it to fuel a popular consumption boom. Appalled by this short-sighted approach, Harold Macmillan, the former prime minister and the grand old man of the Conservative Party, publicly rebuked Thatcher's government. Macmillan likened Thatcher's policy to the actions of an aristocratic family selling off the family silver to fund its elaborate lifestyle: "First of all the Georgian silver goes. And then all that nice furniture that used to be in the salon."[18] Although he never actually used the words, "selling off the family silver" became a popular phrase, a shorthand way of expressing British uneasiness about the quick sale of what had been national possessions. To make matters worse, the family silver seemed to end up in the deep pockets of a very few: many of the executives of the newly privatized companies granted themselves extraordinarily high salaries, which enraged much of the British public, while employment in these companies was often cut by 20 to 40 percent.

Nevertheless, most economists deemed Thatcher's privatization project to be largely an economic success. To prepare the various industries for sale, Thatcher's government injected them with much-needed capital, used for long overdue modernization and mechanization. Thatcher also brought in successful businessmen as new industry heads to overhaul management and production (which often translated into large job losses). As a result, industries entered the private sector "leaner and meaner," able to generate profits for their shareholders and contribute to revitalizing the British economy.

Yet the privatization project was not solely economic in nature. By reducing the nationalized sector of the economy, Thatcher aimed to shrink the role of the state in economic affairs and here privatization proved less successful. In most cases, the privatized industry remained a monopoly, overseen by a government regulatory agency charged with maintaining standards and fair prices. For example, when British Gas was privatized in 1986, the company received a twenty-five-year monopoly on the distribution of gas and a new government agency called Ofgas was created to ensure that prices did not skyrocket and services plummet under private ownership. Similarly, when British Telecom was privatized, Oftel was set up to ensure that the newly private firm kept its price rises below the inflation rate. State ownership of much of the economy disappeared; state control did not.

While privatization became the standard-bearer of the Thatcher Revolution, curbing the power of the trade unions also remained high on Thatcher's agenda. Since World War II, British governments had viewed the trade union movement as a political partner, a key player in managing and regulating the economy. The sight of burly union leaders arriving at the prime minister's residence at Number 10 Downing Street for lengthy meetings to hammer out wage agreements and thereby settle or avoid damaging strikes—summed up in the popular press as "beer and sandwiches at No. 10"—demonstrated the corporatist assumptions of this postwar social democratic settlement. In her second term, Thatcher decisively shattered this corporatist tradition. Legal changes, the symbolically important defeat of the miners' union, and accelerated deindustrialization worked together to gut trade union power.

When Thatcher took office in 1979, she opted for a gradualist approach to trade union reform legislation, moving cautiously along a series of steppingstones. By 1984, this gradual legislative approach was showing results. Two measures, in particular, effectively curbed industrial action. First, unions lost their legal immunities and so were now financially liable for damages caused in unlawful strikes. Second, strikes were legal only if a majority of union members voted in favor of industrial action via a secret ballot.

Even more important than this legislation in gutting trade union power, however, was Thatcher's performance during the coal miners' strike of 1984–1985. Throughout the 1970s, the coal miners' unions wielded immense political clout; in 1974, a miners' strike toppled Heath's government. Defeating the miners' unions was, then, of great political and symbolic significance for Thatcher. In 1981, she formed a secret committee to make national preparations for the next major coal strike. Over the next three years, the government built up a large backup supply of coal for power stations and also devised emergency plans to ensure coal deliveries.

The stage was thus set for a massive confrontation, which began in 1984 when the National Coal Board announced an efficiency drive that mandated the closure of older, less productive pits in Scotland, south Wales, and the North of England. Because "the pit" provided the only employment for men in many villages, these closures were guaranteed to decimate entire communities and so were strongly opposed by the National Union of Miners (NUM). Unlike previous postwar prime ministers, Thatcher refused to call the NUM leaders into 10 Downing Street for negotiations; she recognized that by denying them access, she denied them influence. The NUM ordered its members to the picket lines. With the stakes so high, the strike quickly turned violent. Night after night, British television screens featured memorable scenes of mounted policemen beating back miners who tried to prevent the movement of coal supplies. This sort of footage placed great pressure on the government, but Thatcher refused to budge. "What we have got," she declared, "is an attempt to substitute the rule of the mob for the rule of the law, and it must not succeed."[19]

Fortunately for Thatcher, her emergency preparations proved effective. Even more fortunately, the NUM leader Arthur Scargill was an easy man to defeat. Scargill made no secret of his desire to use union power to overthrow the elected government and ignored both British law and the NUM's own constitution by refusing to allow miners to vote on the strike before it began. When most of the miners in Nottinghamshire, where pits were not scheduled for closure, refused to go on strike, he again broke the law by sending in "flying pickets"—unionists from other regions—to coerce the Nottinghamshire miners into striking. Pictures of miners harassing and even attacking other miners undercut the union's appeal. Even more damaging was the revelation that Scargill had requested financial backing from Muammar Gaddafi, the Libyan dictator and sponsor of global terrorism. By the end of 1984, miners were trickling back to work; defeated, the NUM called off the strike in March of 1985. The strike achieved nothing, except to catapult many striking miners' families into poverty even more quickly than the pit closures would have.

The ongoing deindustrialization of the British economy further diminished trade union power. The transformation from an industrial to postindustrial economy now accelerated to a breathtaking pace, as heavy industry gave way to consumer-driven service industries—many of them small, self-employed ventures, many of them linked to the global telecommunications revolution that was just beginning. The high-wage, low-skilled industrial job, once plentiful, became an endangered species. Many of the jobs that were available were part-time and low-paying and tended to be dominated by women. For steelworkers, coal miners, shipyard hands, textile mill operatives, and the like, particularly if they were men, the 1980s were tough times, marked by declining wages and job insecurity—if they were lucky enough to remain employed. These were also tough times for unions. By 1990, only 37 percent of the workforce was unionized.

During Thatcher's second government, then, Britain offered the Western world a vision of a new sort of society: one that featured both mass unemployment and mass prosperity. By the mid-1980s, the deflationary policies of Chancellors of the Exchequer Geoffrey Howe and Nigel Lawson had borne fruit. With inflation falling below 6 percent, Lawson was able to lower interest rates and ease access to credit. This move, plus the infusion of revenue from privatization and North Sea oil sparked a massive consumer boom. Economic recovery was underway; the average British income rose by 35 percent between 1983 and 1987. The High Streets (equivalent of the American Main Street) of many British cities surged with shoppers and long-time slum areas of London such as the Docklands and Canary Wharf underwent glitzy renovations (achieved, somewhat ironically, with government subsidies).

A key aspect of this economic resurgence was the remarkable renewal of "the City," London's version of Wall Street. One of Thatcher's earliest actions had been to abolish currency exchange controls in October 1979—"arguably," according to John Campbell, "the single most important step the Thatcher Government took to give practical effect to its belief in free markets."[20] Ever since the outbreak of World War II, British governments had regulated the movement of capital to prop up the value of the pound. Abolishing exchange controls meant, in a sense, thrusting the British economy and currency into the global marketplace. It was a daring step—Geoffrey Howe described it as "the only economic decision of my life that ever caused me to lose a night's sleep"—but one made less risky by the flow of North Sea oil which helped keep up the pound's value.[21]

This important step was followed by the Big Bang of October 27, 1986. On a single day, many of the London Stock Exchange's time-honored—but some argued, hopelessly antiquated—traditions and regulations were tossed overboard. The regulations that had sought to ensure that brokers did not profit from dubious trades disappeared, foreign banks and brokers were allowed in, and the old "open out-cry" system of trading gave way to electronic on-screen deals. Transactions that had taken ten minutes now took ten seconds. The Big Bang obliterated a somewhat fusty but familiar world of family firms and old-boy networks, of well-tailored upper-class men wearing bowler hats and carrying furled umbrellas, of long alcohol-fueled midday dinners and deals done on a handshake. New traders poured in, not only from abroad but also from the lower ranks of British society—ambitious working and lower-middle-class men and women willing to work phenomenally long hours in exchange for a chance at phenomenally high salaries and bonuses. Reinvigorated by the new blood and new technology, the London stock market, which had been falling behind its competitors in New York, Tokyo, and Frankfurt, reclaimed its historic role as the global financial leader. By 1987, the City's volume of trading was fifteen times higher than it had been in the early 1980s. By the 1990s, 520 foreign banks from 76 countries conducted more foreign-exchange transactions in London than in any city in the world.[22]

Many of the firms that benefited, however, were not British. As a result of the Big Bang, London became the capital of a multinational economy that made nonsense of national borders. In this way, then, Thatcher's policies led in a direction she had not intended or desired. Always a strong British nationalist, Thatcher identified the defense of what she believed to be unique British strengths and unique British values as a key component of Thatcherism. Yet under her governance Britain became much more thoroughly enmeshed in not only the European but the global economy, and London in particular grew ever more multicultural, less a British than an international city. A similar sort of irony can be observed in another result of the Big Bang and the financial boom it sparked. In this new world—where fortunes could be made, or lost, literally overnight—traditional British reserve gave way to the celebration of conspicuous consumption. A new materialism, an obsession with getting and spending money, clashed with, and to a large degree triumphed over, values such as thrift and prudence that Thatcher most cherished.

One of the central features of the economic boom during the second half of the 1980s was, in fact, a colossal expansion of consumer debt. The deregulation of what the British call "hire purchase" (installment buying), increases in the tax deduction for mortgage interest, and easy credit all encouraged spending. The average level of personal indebtedness rose almost four times as fast as the average income, a paradoxical development under a prime minister who disapproved of credit cards and sought to develop habits of hard work and saving for tomorrow. An important technological innovation both symbolized and accentuated this new spendthrift society: the Automatic Teller Machine or ATM—in British English, "the hole-in-the-wall"—gave the consuming masses twenty-four-hour access to their bank accounts.

And once they had drawn their pound notes from the hole-in-the-wall, shoppers frequently bought goods made abroad. By 1986, consumption of imported goods stood at twice what it had been in 1979. In contrast, British manufacturing in 1986 had only just regained its levels of 1979. Nevertheless, Thatcher's governments—unlike her predecessors'—did not have to

VISIT TO LANCASHIRE BISCUIT (COOKIE) FACTORY, MAY 1987. *By the time Thatcher toured this factory in May of 1987, the manufacturing capacity of Lancashire and other northern counties had contracted dramatically.*

grapple with balance-of-payments crises. The revenues from North Sea oil made up for the gap between income from exports and outgo on imports. Industrial investment, however, stood at 16 percent less in 1986 than in 1979—and North Sea oil was not limitless.[23] Thatcher's economic renovation, then, did not rest on an entirely firm foundation.

Moreover, not all Britons participated in the economic boom. The number of people in poverty doubled between 1979 and 1987.[24] The key factor here was unemployment, which remained above the 3 million mark until the autumn of 1986, when it finally began to decline. Not until 1989, however, did the numbers of unemployed fall below 2 million. One of the most revolutionary aspects of the Thatcher Revolution, then, was to shatter the postwar social democratic commitment to maintaining full employment. From 1945 on, both Labour and Conservative leaders assumed that a high rate of unemployment was socially and politically unsustainable: They agreed that mass joblessness destroyed social cohesion and threatened to undermine democratic values, and that the electorate simply would not tolerate the return of 1930s' style joblessness. The Thatcher Revolution made mass unemployment acceptable. Thatcher's second Chancellor of the Exchequer Nigel Lawson stated baldly, "Economically and politically Britain can get along with double-digit unemployment."[25]

By the end of Thatcher's second term, the gap between rich and poor, the haves and the have-nots, was widening. Thatcher herself did not regard inequality as a bad thing. In her eyes, social inequality served as an engine of economic growth by compelling the ambitious to take risks to gain a spot at the top of the social ladder. As she put it in a famous speech (given to an American audience), "Opportunity means nothing unless it includes the right to be unequal. Let our children grow tall, and some grow taller than others if they have it in them to do so."[26] Like the American president Ronald Reagan, Thatcher believed that enhancing the wealth of the top sectors of society would, eventually, enrich all of society; wealth would "trickle down." But this trickle never made it down to the very poor. During the 1980s, the incomes of the wealthiest 10 percent of the British population rose by over 60 percent. In contrast, the incomes of the poorest 10 percent dropped by 17 percent.[27]

Thatcher's taxation policies, devised not to redistribute income to the have-nots but rather to reward the haves, helped widen the gap between rich and poor. Although Thatcher spoke frequently about the need to cut taxes and liberate the taxpayer, taxation actually accounted for a larger percentage of the GDP at the end of her years in office than it had at the beginning: from 38.5 percent in 1979 to over 40 percent in 1990. What changed was not so much the *amount* of revenue collected as *how* it was collected—and *from whom*. The wealthy benefited from the cut in the top rate of income tax—reduced to 60 percent in Thatcher's first government, to 40 percent in Thatcher's third—and reduction of capital gains and inheritance taxes. Moreover, despite her determination to reduce the size and expense of government, Thatcher insisted on what she termed "socially desirable" state expenditure, a category that included tax relief for people paying a mortgage on their home, for parents of children in private schools, and for buyers of private health insurance plans. People on the bottom end of the economic scale, however, did not usually own their own home, send their children to private schools, or opt out of the NHS. They had low income levels, nothing for their children to inherit, and no capital on which to gain. For these people, the Thatcherist policy of shifting revenue from direct (income and payroll deduction) to indirect (sales) taxes hit much harder.

The Thatcher Revolution also widened Britain's regional divide. The South benefited from not only the revitalization of the financial sector but also the telecommunications revolution and the expansion of service-oriented industries. In the North, however, where mass industrial unemployment was concentrated, economic prospects remained bleak. In some Northern cities—such as Manchester, Sheffield, and Glasgow, once the showcases of the Industrial Revolution—youth unemployment reached 50 percent. Unemployment in Scotland stood 25 percent higher than in the United Kingdom as a whole.[28]

Britons remained divided in their assessment of Thatcher's ongoing revolution. To Conservative grassroots activists, Thatcher stood second only to Winston Churchill in their pantheon of national heroes. She had brought Britain back into global prominence and she had reversed the nation's economic decline. Inflation was down. The unions had been politically weakened and strikes were at an all-time low. More people owned their own homes than ever before. The economy was growing at between 2.5 and 3 percent a year. These supporters agreed wholeheartedly with Thatcher's own assessment: "Seven years ago, who would have dared forecast such a transformation of Britain? This didn't come about because of consensus. It happened because we said: This we believe, this we will do. It's called leadership."[29]

Yet not everyone was convinced. A wave of rioting throughout British cities in the autumn of 1985 demonstrated serious social discontent. Some critics charged that Thatcher's social policies had incited the riots; others blamed her not being tough enough on crime. Thatcher herself blamed the "culture of excuses" that she believed had flourished in the fertile soil of the permissive society. Insisting that there was "no excuse, no justification whatever for the riots," she cracked down with a Public Order Act that expanded police resources for riot control, as well as a Criminal Justice Act that imposed longer sentences on criminals, provided compensation to victims of crime, and limited the ability of defense attorneys to challenge jurors.[30] Her efforts to reintroduce capital punishment, however, were defeated.

While most of those rioting in the summer of 1985 came from the lower social classes, Thatcher also encountered sharp hostility at the other end of the social spectrum, in traditional citadels of power and privilege. The same year that looters were ransacking British city centers, Oxford University faculty voted, by a margin of two to one, to deny Thatcher the honorary doctorate traditionally given to prime ministers. It was a calculated and very public insult, meant to demonstrate academia's outrage at Thatcherist policies, particularly her slash-and-burn approach to the universities. Universities suffered a 20 percent cut in funding and, in consequence, reductions in the numbers of students, programs, and faculty. In 1985, another powerful traditional institution, the Church of England, also broadcast its discontent with Thatcher in a report called "Faith in the City." This well-publicized report argued that Thatcher's policies had worsened social inequality and deepened urban blight. It concluded, "A growing number of people are excluded by poverty or powerlessness from sharing in the common life of our nation."[31]

The general election of 1987 illustrated the growing divisions within Britain. On the one hand, it was a Conservative landslide, with Thatcher's party sweeping the South and the Tories winning 397 seats in Parliament to Labour's 209 and the Alliance's 23. Thatcher had now led her party to three major electoral victories. On the other hand, the Conservatives won only 42 percent of the popular vote and lost seats in the North of England, Wales, and Scotland. If we equate supporters of the Thatcher Revolution with those who cast their votes for the Conservative Party, then only 31 percent of the electorate stood behind Thatcherism. An opinion poll taken the same year found that 61 percent of the British public preferred higher taxes and better public services, including welfare, to the lower taxes and privatized society offered by Thatcherism.[32]

|THATCHER'S DEFEAT: 1987–1990|

ON THE EVENING OF NOVEMBER 20, 1990, in the glittering halls of the Palace of Versailles, the champagne flowed, course after course of lavishly prepared food appeared on the tables, and the world's most powerful men and women—American president George H. W. Bush, French premier François Mitterand, German chancellor Helmut Kohl, Soviet leader Mikhail Gorbachev, and, of course, Margaret Thatcher—celebrated the signing of what Thatcher described as the "biggest international disarmament agreement since the end of the last World War," an agreement that in fact heralded the end of the cold war.[1] The communist regimes of Eastern Europe had fallen and were now moving rapidly to reduce the state's presence in their economies. The cold war was over, and Thatcher herself could rightly claim to have contributed to this fundamental reshaping of the world order. She should, then, have been on top of the world that November evening. And yet, just hours earlier, the members of the Conservative parliamentary party had voted to replace her as party leader—and thus as Britain's prime minister. Her fellow dinner guests were amazed that a woman who had won three general elections and who possessed a commanding parliamentary majority could be pushed out of office by members of her own party.

Back in Britain, however, amazement mingled with relief and, in many sectors, exultation. In 1987, Thatcher briskly began her third government in a much weaker position than was readily apparent even, or perhaps especially, to her. Although Conservative grassroots activists adored her, Thatcher's authoritarian style of governing had over the years alienated many members of the Conservative parliamentary party, particularly within the Cabinet-level ranks. Moreover, outside the walls of Westminster and the ranks of the party, dissatisfaction with Thatcher was intense. After a decade of Thatcherism, large sections of the British population opposed key facets of the Thatcher Revolution. Yet the prime minister shrugged off the warning signs and moved ahead with policies that proved deeply unpopular, even among many of her fiercest supporters. Now a star on the world stage, Thatcher failed to see that many in the audience at home had stopped applauding.

The applause abroad, however, kept building. By the time Thatcher won her third general election in June, 1987, the stage was set in Eastern Europe for riveting drama, as Poles and Hungarians led the way in rewriting the script of international politics. As stagflation hit the already faltering Eastern European economies in the early 1980s, public discontent mounted; the pressure for radical political as well as economic change grew intense. Thatcher visited Poland in November 1988. Such a visit at such a time had consequences. Polish anti-communist activists regarded the Iron Lady as a fellow freedom fighter and saw her visit as a declaration of support, a view solidified by Thatcher's insistence that she meet with the leaders of Solidarity, the still illegal anti-communist political movement. Everywhere she went, admiring Polish crowds shouted "*Vivat* Thatcher!"[2]

Just a few weeks later, Soviet leader Mikhael Gorbachev gave a revolutionary speech in the United Nations in which he announced drastic unilateral cuts in Soviet military forces in Eastern Europe and made it clear that the Soviet satellite states were now free to choose their own political path. In the early months of 1989, Hungary legalized non-Communist political parties and trade unions and Polish communist officials sat down with members of Solidarity for talks aimed at restructuring Poland's political system. In June, Poland held the first free elections in the Soviet bloc. Solidarity swept the contest and formed the first non-Communist government in Eastern Europe since 1948. By the time Thatcher stood up at the Conservative Party conference in October to give her usual speech, crescendoing protests in Hungary, East Germany, Czechoslovakia, and Romania spelled the end of communism in Eastern Europe.

Thatcher had always viewed her battles against social democracy at home and communism abroad as part of the same war and so she did not hesitate to link these events to the Thatcher Revolution: "The messages on our banners in 1979—freedom, opportunity, family, enterprise, ownership—are now inscribed on the banners in Leipzig, Warsaw, Budapest and even Moscow." To the Conservative faithful gathered at the party's annual

BEFORE THE FALL. *Thatcher stands triumphant at the Conservative Party Conference in October 1989. A year later, Conservative MPs would remove her from office. Her successor, John Major, stands just behind Thatcher's right hand.*

conference in 1989, Thatcher declared, "We did not know it at the time, but the torch we lit in Britain . . . became a beacon that has shed its light across the Iron Curtain into the East."[3] A year later, she visited Hungary and Czechoslovakia, both now under non-Communist governments. Enthusiastic crowds greeted her at every stop and made it clear that they saw her as, in biographer John Campbell's words, a "living embodiment of anti-Communism."[4]

The euphoria generated by the Revolutions of 1989 was very real, as was Thatcher's sense that she had helped make these events happen. The ensuing development, however, alarmed her deeply. After the opening of the Berlin Wall in November of 1989 and its subsequent dismantling, West German chancellor Helmut Kohl began to push hard for the reunification of East and West Germany. Thatcher was horrified. She feared that a single Germany would upset the European balance of power and thereby threaten to undermine Gorbachev's reform efforts in the Soviet Union. These fears were not baseless: Gorbachev's domestic position was increasingly shaky. But underneath such arguments lay gut emotion—Thatcher's visceral mistrust of Germany and Germans. In unguarded moments, her prejudice against Germans came to the fore: "We've been through the war and we know perfectly well what the Germans are like, and what dictators can do, and how national character doesn't basically change."[5]

Convinced that German reunification spelled disaster for all of Europe, Thatcher fought hard to block Kohl and slow the pace of events. She found herself, however, almost completely isolated. Few British diplomats shared her views; even more important, she no longer had a receptive ear at the White House. George H. W. Bush had replaced Reagan at the start of 1989; although a Republican and generally in agreement with Thatcherism, Bush did not share Reagan's great affection for Thatcher. Moreover, because he had served as Reagan's vice president, he needed to establish some distance between his own policies and those of his predecessor. And perhaps most crucially, Thatcher in 1989 was not the same as the Thatcher who had welcomed Reagan's election in 1981. She had grown accustomed to telling people what to do—not, of course, the best approach to an American president. In October 1990, less than one year after the Berlin Wall was opened, East and West Germany joined in a united state, with Kohl as chancellor.

The divide between Bush and Thatcher over German reunification did not, however, alter Thatcher's essential Atlanticism. She remained convinced that British interests lay in marching in step with the Americans, as the First Gulf War (also known as Operation Desert Storm) demonstrated. In August 1990, Iraqi dictator Saddam Hussein sent troops into neighboring Kuwait. It was an unprovoked act of aggression against a peaceful state; even more alarming was the chance that Iraqi forces would push through Kuwait into Saudi Arabia, home to 60 percent of the world's oil reserves. On the day of the invasion, Thatcher was in Aspen, Colorado, awaiting a long-arranged meeting with the American president. Thatcher did not hesitate to pledge full British support for a military coalition to drive Iraq out of Kuwait. She called for immediate and resolute action: "If we let [the invasion of Kuwait] succeed, no small country can ever feel safe again. The law of the jungle would take over from the rule of law."[6] She did not have the same relationship with Bush as she had had with Reagan, but over the next several months Thatcher worked closely with the American president in assembling the coalition and obtaining approval from the United Nations for military action. During one phone call between the two leaders at the end of August, she uttered the words that became a kind of mantra in the Bush administration: Iraqi oil tankers were trying to beat the Allied blockade and Bush called Thatcher to tell her that— against her advice—he had decided to delay firing on the ships. She reluctantly agreed but added, "This is no time to go wobbly."[7] Bush did not go wobbly and the Allied coalition, including 45,000 British troops, drove Iraq out of Kuwait.

Applauded on the world stage, Thatcher saw no reason not to push her way forward on the domestic platform as well. Delighted by the election results of 1987, she told a television interviewer, "We have just had the most fantastic triumph." She made it clear that she had no intention of resting on her laurels. When asked if she had any plans to groom a successor, she dismissed the idea out of hand, "Good heavens, no."[8] In her speech to the Conservative Party Conference that autumn, Thatcher insisted that this third election victory "was only a staging post on a much longer journey," and boasted, "'Can't be done' has given way to 'What's to stop us?'"[9] In Thatcher's third term, then, more radical privatization, the reorganization of the National Health Service, and substantial changes in social security and in education characterized the ongoing Thatcher Revolution. Public opposition in each of these four areas, however, helped erode Thatcher's hold on her party.

Privatization, the keystone of Thatcher's second government, continued after 1987, with the British Airports Authority, British Petroleum, British Steel, and the Rolls Royce car company all shifting from public to private ownership. As with the earlier denationalization of significant industries, these privatizations were hailed as economic successes, a crucial contribution to the Thatcher economic revival that saw the British GDP expand between 1985 and 1989 by 14.5 percent. In her third term, however, Thatcher extended the privatization project into the more contentious area of public utilities. Unlike companies like Rolls Royce, British Petroleum, or British Steel, the water and electricity industries had never been in private hands. Water had been under municipal control since the nineteenth century and the creation of the electricity grid had been a state achievement. Perhaps not surprisingly, then, the privatization of electricity and water proved deeply unpopular. In a poll in 1996, for example, the privatized utility companies stood at the top of the public's "most hated" list.[10] The fact that essential, and essentially communal, resources were now items of private property appalled many Britons, and rising utility bills—the average water bill jumped up by 40 percent—infuriated many more. So, too, did falling standards of service, particularly when compared to the skyrocketing salaries of the new utility CEOs. Nevertheless, there was little talk of "renationalization." Thatcher had irrevocably reshaped Britain's entire economic landscape. By 1990, forty state-owned companies had been privatized and approximately 600,000 people who had worked for the state no longer did so.[11]

National health care, however, remained an enormous state enterprise. Thatcher recognized that privatizing the National Health Service (NHS) was politically impossible; her administrative overhaul of the NHS in her second term had already cost her a great deal of political capital. Poll after poll during the general election showed that the condition of the NHS topped the list of voters' concerns. Headlines about staff shortages, delayed operations, long waiting lists, and even deaths created an atmosphere of crisis, and much of the public blamed Thatcher. Spending on the NHS had fallen during her second term and remained below the western European norm.

Convinced that the NHS wasted taxpayers' money, Thatcher was determined to subject the service to what she regarded as the bracing discipline of the free marketplace. She announced that she personally would chair a review of the NHS. The resulting report, published in January 1989, mandated a set of changes aimed at "stimulating within the NHS as many as possible of the advantages which the private sector and market choice offered, but without privatization."[12] The "purchaser-provider split" formed the basis of these changes. Rather than hospitals and doctors billing the state for services rendered, the central government would now issue lump sums to district health authorities (the "purchasers"), which would then contract with hospitals and doctors (the "providers") across the country for necessary services. In addition, the new system encouraged doctors to form their own "purchasing" units by splitting off from the district, receiving funds directly from the central state, and shopping around for the best services, specialists, and hospital care for their patients. Within the confines of the NHS, then, an "internal market" would operate. The free hand of competition would slap the NHS into shape by rewarding the most skilled and efficient and by eliminating the wasteful and incompetent.

In an ironic twist, these reforms strengthened the NHS but weakened Thatcher. Polls showed that the British public over-whelmingly believed that the NHS was not safe in Thatcher's hands; people realized that in the ideal Thatcherist world, the NHS would not exist. As a result, the reforms generated a public outcry. The British Medical Association led the charge against the plan with a poster campaign across the country. In a play on the words often applied to the stationing of American troops in Britain during World War II ("overpaid, oversexed, and over here"), it declared that the NHS was "underfunded, undermined, and under threat."[13] Many critics argued that the internal market was a fiction, that patients were not consumers shopping around the country for the best medical deal. A sick person wanted to see a local doctor and to use a local hospital. As with the privatization of utilities, however, the reforms went ahead and by the mid-1990s, even her critics concluded that more patients received better care because Thatcher had wrought "a real change in the management of the NHS without undermining its principle."[14] Yet by the mid-1990s, Thatcher was long out of office; in the short run, taking on the NHS—a service dear to the hearts and pocket-books of her middle-class base—proved politically unpopular.

Social security reforms also proved very controversial. Much to the frustration of Thatcher and her supporters, social security spending had actually risen during her years in office and by her third term accounted for one-third of total government spending (largely because of high unemployment, which of course trans-lated into high levels of spending on unemployment benefits). Much as she would have liked to reduce this figure radically, Thatcher found herself constrained by practical politics. For example, al-though she loathed the universal child benefit allowance—she declared it "absurd" that well-to-do families received state aid—she recognized that even "our people" (middle-class homeowners) regarded the allowance as a right rather than a handout.[15] Instead of eliminating the allowance as she would have preferred, therefore, Thatcher froze its value so that it would slowly dwindle to insignificance as part of a family budget.

In general, Thatcher's reforms that went into effect in 1988 sought to shift the emphasis of British social security programs from universal provision to something more along the lines of what Americans call "welfare." The reforms also sought to shift resources from the unemployed and single young adults—whom Thatcher tended to regard as scroungers—to those she deemed deserving of state assistance: families with young children, the aged, and the disabled. Thatcher insisted that those who gained far outnumbered those who lost, but the statistics showed otherwise. Approximately 60 to 80 percent of recipients of assistance proved to be worse off after the reforms. At the same time, Thatcher's government reduced the top level of income tax from 60 to 40 percent. The juxtaposition of this action with cuts to benefits for the poor enraged many observers. Overall, controversy surrounding the changes in social security reinforced the popular sense of a government that had gone too far and a prime minister that had governed too long.

In terms of parliamentary hours consumed, Thatcher's education reforms proved even more contentious. The Great Education Reform Bill (Gerbil, for short) of 1988 set a postwar record by taking up 370 hours of parliamentary time. A colossal piece of legislation, Gerbil sought to change what was taught, how it was taught, and who controlled the schools and universities in which it was taught. Gerbil's centerpiece was a National Curriculum for England and Wales (Scotland controlled its own schools and universities). At the start of the reform process, Thatcher envisioned that this curriculum would consist of a simple set of standards and targets in what she considered the three "core" subjects of English, mathematics, and science, but as the bill made its way through the legislative process, it grew considerably more complex and rather ridiculous. The central government, rather than teachers or local education authorities, now dictated learning targets and class-time allocation for not only the three "core" subjects but also seven "foundation" subjects (history, geography, technology, art, music, a foreign language, and religious education), with pupils' performance on national standardized tests (at ages seven, eleven, fourteen, and sixteen) bearing witness to a school's success in meeting these standards. The act was not implemented until after Thatcher left office, but by becoming personally involved in many of the details of the curriculum, particularly the content of the history syllabus (she believed history teaching should emphasize great British men, great British battles, and lots of great British dates), she once again squandered precious political capital as not only teachers and teachers' unions but also middle-class parents expressed uneasiness with the new educational system that was taking shape.

The National Curriculum epitomized the most ironic, and one of the most important, aspects of the Thatcher Revolution. Despite Thatcher's pledge to free individuals from the demands of an overly mighty state, Thatcherism vastly increased the power of the central government, multiplied the number of bureaucrats, and generated piles and piles of paperwork. The irony deepens when we look at the history of the Conservative Party, which evolved out of local gentry's mistrust of strong central rule and which had long championed local interests against London. In British politics, Conservatives were seen as the traditionalists, the defenders of regional diversity and provincial peculiarities. Yet Thatcher's Conservative Governments sought to create uniform regulations across the country and stripped local governments of much of their authority and most of their funding. Thatcher's personal history deepens the irony even more. She proclaimed herself to be her father's daughter; she constantly acknowledged his shaping influence and insisted that the lessons she learned in his grocery store formed the fundamental principles of her politics. Yet Alfred Roberts devoted his life to local government and civic volunteerism; under Thatcher, local government declined significantly in autonomy and influence, while the civic sense dwindled.

Frequently this centralization of power was an unintended byproduct of Thatcher's faith in the free market, as the Education Act of 1988 illustrates. Thatcher backed the act because she believed it would create a competitive educational marketplace: The act encouraged schools to separate themselves from the control of the local education authority and instead receive funding directly from the central government. In Thatcher's vision, the best schools, freed of the burden of local governmental misman-agement, would attract students while failing schools would be forced to shape up or shut down. The schools that opted out of local control, however, were not allowed to manage their own finances or set their own priorities; the central state claimed that power.

Centralization not only diminished local independence; it also created new bureaucracies—another unintended and para-doxical result of Thatcher's effort to reduce government interven-tion. The Education Act again exemplifies this process. The act stripped control of their finances from universities and gave this power to a new Universities Funding Council—whose members were state appointees. Mandated to distribute funds based on "performance," the council members effectively controlled uni-versity teaching and research throughout the country. Assessing the performance of teachers and researchers across diverse disci-plines proved highly problematic, however; the Council began by counting books and articles, then pages, then citations in other scholarly works as it scrambled to find some form of standard-ized, quantitative measurement. All of this counting and assess-ing required counters and assessors. As the ranks of bureaucratic overseers grew, they gobbled up scarce financial resources and thus performance demands on, and budget cuts to, the universi-ties grew even more stringent.

The waning of local autonomy under Thatcher occurred not only as an unintended result of her economic reforms but also as a very intentional consequence of her war against socialism. Many local governments, particularly in large cities, were controlled by Labour—and in some instances, by the so-called looney Left. These left-wing activists in the Labour Party agreed with Thatcher that social democratic politics had failed; unlike Thatcher, they believed that Britain needed to move in a more thoroughly socialist direction. Ken Livingstone, the leader of the Greater London Council (GLC) led the charge. Under "Red Ken," the GLC (which oversaw all the London boroughs) increased its expenditures by 170 percent in just five years, subsidized a variety of social and cultural groups (sometimes by putting supporters onto the city payroll), used taxpayers' money for political propaganda against Thatcher and, perhaps most provocatively, posted the growing number of London unemployed on a giant banner on the front of the council building, just across the Thames River from the House of Commons. After struggling for a number of years to rein in Red Ken and his like, Thatcher took the drastic step of abolishing the GLC and seventeen other urban councils. A number of these councils, like the GLC, were high-spending and rife with corruption, but by abolishing them unilaterally, Thatcher not only removed democratically elected bodies from the political process, she also expanded the responsibilities and augmented the power of the central state.

In Thatcher's eyes, moreover, Red Ken epitomized *all* local government, not just socialist-led, spendthrift, big-city councils. Even Conservative-held local councils were, she believed, prone to waste and inefficiency, apt to lavish their constituents with costly services. As a result, Thatcher's governments passed more than fifty Acts of Parliament that diminished local governmental autonomy and, by default, consolidated power in the hands of the central state.[16] "Right-to-buy" housing legislation, for example, forced local councils to sell their housing stock at discount rates to their more prosperous tenants and forbade them to construct more public housing. Other measures required local governments to privatize services such as street cleaning and trash collection, while the changes in the NHS meant that local control of hospitals diminished sharply. In 1984, councils lost the power to set their own budgets and thus the ability to determine their own priorities. And across the board, a series of new schemes—for neighborhood redevelopment, youth training, housing associations, and the like—were placed in the hands of the central government itself or of government-appointed agencies with no accountability to the localities they actually served.

It was Thatcher's struggle to rein in local government that propelled her into one of the most damaging episodes of her career. The *poll tax*, as it came to be known, weakened Thatcher's support even among her middle-class base and set the stage for the Conservative parliamentary party to remove her from office in 1990. The poll tax debacle originated in Thatcher's effort to abolish the "rates." In the British system, the rates constituted a local property tax paid by businesses and homeowners to fund part of the costs of local government. Hostility toward rate-paying had long been a feature of Conservative politics and had in fact been a central theme of the young Margaret Roberts' first parliamentary campaigns in Dartford in the early 1950s. The basis of this hostility was simple: Only property owners paid rates. Of 35 million voters in England in the early 1980s, 18 million paid rates; 6 million paid a reduced rate or had their rate paid by their housing benefit; the remaining 11 million paid nothing.[17] Yet everyone, of course, benefited from local governmental services such as street cleaning, road maintenance, and library provisions. Moreover, Conservatives had long argued, those who paid nothing—renters and people on the lower end of the economic scale—benefited more than the property owners who did pay from such services as council housing and public transport. They also argued that because non-rate-payers had no vested interest in keeping the rates low, they had no compunction about pushing for additional and costly local services; after all, they would never see the bill. Hence, the entire system of local government, for Thatcher, violated the proper order of things: individuals should pay for the services they received.

The problem of the rates intensified throughout the 1980s because Thatcher's policies squeezed local governments' budgets. When Thatcher took office, only about 40 percent of local government revenue came from the rates, with grants from the central government supplying the remaining 60 percent. By 1988, however, the figures had flip-flopped; only about 40 percent of local expenditures were paid by the center. As the revenue flow from the center dwindled, local authorities turned up their other faucet; that is, they raised the rates.

During Thatcher's first two governments, she and her advisers struggled to find an adequate substitute for the rates. The obvious alternative, a local income tax, was deeply unpopular with the Conservative base and violated Thatcher's core convictions. She hated the way an income tax redistributed wealth and believed that such a tax punished individuals who worked hard. Other ideas, such as local sales taxes or simply a central government takeover of local government services, proved problematic. After the general election of 1987, therefore, Thatcher decided to move ahead with the poll tax—or as it was officially labeled, the *community charge*.

The plan for the poll tax was breathtaking in its simplicity: Every individual over the age of eighteen must pay a uniform community charge. Every adult in a community, in other words, would pay the same amount. There were some exceptions—students would pay a lower rate and a system of means-tested rebates was intended to reduce the burden on those unable to pay—but in general the community charge was, as the common term made clear, a poll (or head) tax. The amount paid did not depend on income earned, purchases made, property owned, or work performed. It was a simple, uniform charge. Local councils were to set the amount for each community. People with a high poll tax would soon realize, Thatcher argued, that "they have grossly extravagant local authorities"—and would, she assumed, use the power of the ballot box to curb that extravagance and reduce the tax.[18] Meanwhile, the poll tax plan called for a single national business rate to be collected by the central government and redistributed to local governments on a per capita basis—another example of the centralizing and standardizing tendencies of Thatcherism.

First introduced in Scotland in 1989, the poll tax aroused immediate and intense opposition, including riotous protests and widespread refusal to comply with the law. Nevertheless, Thatcher moved ahead with applying the poll tax in England and Wales, against the advice of many in her Cabinet and party. Conservatives such as Sir George Young, who had served as a junior minister in Thatcher's Cabinet from 1981 to 1986, pointed out the basic unfairness of a plan under which he would see his payment fall from £2,000 to £300 per year while others in much less comfortable circumstances would pay as much as he did, or more.[19] In March 1990, poll tax assessments arrived in households. Two years earlier, the government had assured voters that the maximum poll tax per household would be about £200. Instead, poll taxes averaged £400 per household. Over 90 percent of taxpayers paid more under the new system than under the old. Some people suddenly found themselves confronted with charges as high as £1,000–£1,500. As in Scotland, protests erupted throughout England and Wales. One massive demonstration in Trafalgar Square turned so violent that 450 people were injured, including 300 police officers. Thatcher regarded the rioting as "wickedness" and the result of the culture of dependency she had long crusaded against: "A whole class of people—an 'underclass' if you will—had been dragged back into the ranks of responsible society and asked to become not just dependents but citizens; their response was to riot."[20]

But it was not just the denizens of a dependent underclass who protested against the poll tax. Significantly, middle-class homeowners and business interests added their voices to the overwhelming chorus of opposition. As one of Thatcher's ministers put it, the poll tax was "targeted like an Exocet missile" on middle-class households.[21] Thatcher had assumed that taxpayers would direct their anger about high community charges at local authorities; instead, it all came flaming down on her. The anger was so intense that Thatcher's government resorted to additional subsidies for local governments to allow lower poll tax rates. These extra subsidies, plus the cost of administering a charge that people were determined not to pay, cost the state an estimated additional £4 billion over just one year.[22] A financial and political fiasco, the poll tax weakened Thatcher's standing with her middle-class base and convinced many Conservative MPs that the prime minister's finely tuned political antennae had been disabled by her many years in power and that if she remained at the top, the party would lose the next general election.

While the poll tax damaged Thatcher's standing with ordinary voters, it was her growing hostility toward the European Community (EC) that turned the party elite—and many of Britain's financial and commercial interests—against her. Thatcher's Europhobia actually resonated with many Britons: the Conservative Party remained deeply divided on the issue of EC membership, and 50 percent of the British public shared Thatcher's skepticism about its benefits.[23] Nevertheless, tensions between Thatcher and her pro-European financial ministers highlighted the negative consequences of the prime minister's authoritarian governing style and convinced many Conservative MPs that the time had come for Thatcher to step down.

Although Thatcher's colleagues had always found her difficult, antagonisms within the government grew particularly intense during Thatcher's third term. Never one to back down from an argument, she now became less and less likely even to hear, let alone consider, dissenting points of view. She had grown used to having her own way. And she had grown tired. The years of little sleep and no time off had drained even Thatcher's legendary reserves of energy. As angry tirades became more and more part of her governing style, the number of once-loyal supporters who

Daily Express Cartoon: Smacking. *Playing off a proposal to make smacking (spanking) illegal in the United Kingdom, this cartoon highlights Thatcher's less-than-collegial governing style.*

were now hurt, alienated, angered, or just plain fed-up grew. No fewer than fifteen Cabinet ministers had been sacked during her years in power. And perhaps even more significantly, Thatcher had long since abandoned her once-regular visits to the House of Commons tearoom. In her early years as party leader and as prime minister, she had made it a point to know her backbenchers by name, to charm them, to make them feel cosseted and cared for. But by the end of the 1980s she had become a remote figure who simply assumed their support—a dangerous assumption indeed.

The crisis over Britain's role in the EC focused on three issues: Thatcher's fears of a European "superstate" centered at EC headquarters in Brussels, her rejection of the social agenda of the EC, and her opposition to a common European currency. In 1986, Thatcher had helped engineer the Single European Act, which she regarded as clearing the way for a genuine free economic market in Europe. This act, however, also set into motion the transformation of the European *Community* into the European *Union*, a political as well as an economic entity, with its own parliament, defense force, justice system, social legislation, common passport, and common currency. Thatcher's emphatic disapproval of this transformation put her on a collision course with other European leaders, particularly Jacques Delors, president of the European Commission from 1985 to 1995. In 1988, Delors predicted in a speech to the European Parliament that within ten years, "80 percent of the laws affecting the economy and social policy would be passed at a European and not a national level."[24] Such a prediction horrified Thatcher, who declared, "We have not successfully rolled back the frontiers of the State in Britain, only to see them reimposed at a European level with a European super-state exercising a new dominance from Brussels."[25]

Thatcher's fear of a European "super-state" rested on her belief that Continental and British political traditions and identities diverged sharply, as well as on her contempt for social democracy. Ignoring the centralizing tendencies of her own policies and programs, she insisted that Continental Europeans were much more accustomed to and inclined toward the central regulatory state. According to the Thatcherist historical narrative, it had fallen to Britain to defeat absolutism, limit the powers of kings, invent parliamentary democracy, and champion individual freedom. Thatcher viewed her own achievements as part and parcel of this historical sweep. Once again it had been Britain—led by Thatcher herself—that led the way in casting off the tyranny of the social democratic state. But now, Thatcher believed, Delors wanted to recreate that state and reimpose that tyranny under the guise of the European Union. To the Conservative faithful gathered in Brighton for the party's annual conference in 1988 Thatcher promised, "We haven't worked all these years to free Britain from the paralysis of Socialism only to see it creeping in through the back door of central control and bureaucracy in Brussels."[26]

Thatcher's fears of a European "super-state" were reinforced by the European Social Charter. As part of the move toward the European Union, the European Commission at the end of 1988 announced that "the single market should not be regarded as a goal in itself." Instead, there must be a "social dimension" to the Union.[27] Delors spelled out this social dimension in a speech to the British Trades Unions Congress that same year when he called for the harmonization and standardization of working hours and conditions, as well as collective bargaining rights, across the member states. Again, Thatcher was aghast. To her, the Social Charter was simply a "Socialist Charter," a way for unions to regain the powers they had lost under her governments and a means of state interference with the free market.

The Labour Party's embrace of the Social Charter, and of the European Union in general, further intensified Thatcher's hostility toward both. Like the Conservative Party, Labour had long been divided on the issue of Britain's role within the EC. In 1967, it was a Labour government that had fostered Britain's second failed attempt to join the EC but British trade unions—a key component of the Labour Party—tended to view the Community as a capitalist-led cabal that sought to promote the free market at the expense of the worker. In 1975, for example, representatives at a Labour conference, dominated by Britain's two largest unions, voted almost 2:1 to leave the EC. By 1980, hostility toward Europe had made it onto the party manifesto, which called for Britain to withdraw from the EC. Three general election defeats in a row, however, caused a massive rethink of many Labour policies and positions, including its anti-European stance. By the end of the 1980s, Labour was moving toward a firm pro-Europe platform, a move that the Social Charter accelerated. Trade unionists and Labour activists welcomed the Social Charter for the same reasons that Thatcher condemned it: they saw it as a guarantee of workers' rights against a hostile Thatcherist state. Labour's new pro-European outlook could only deepen Thatcher's suspicions of Delors and the Social Charter. For her, the choice was simple: a Common Market, "a Europe based on the widest possible freedom for enterprise," or the European Union, "a Europe governed by Socialist methods of centralized control and regulation."[28]

As important as Thatcher's fears of a European super-state and the Social Charter were in solidifying her antagonism toward Europe, in the end, it all came down to money, money in its most literal sense—the 20-pound note, the thick golden pound coin, the hexagonal silver 50-p, the thin copper penny, all bearing the silhouette of Queen Elizabeth. Thatcher's determination to "save the pound," to preserve Britain's national currency, drove the deepest wedge between her and members of her Cabinet and led directly to her fall from power. For Thatcher, a single common European currency made no economic sense; more broadly, by defending the British pound she was defending Britain, or at least her version of Britain, and British identity.

Thatcher's battle for the pound needs to be set within a context of financial crisis. In the late 1980s, the Thatcherist miracle began to look rather less miraculous. Declining oil revenues, the long-term failure to improve British manufacturing competitiveness, and consumers' continuing appetite for imported goods all added up to a return of trade deficits. Even more alarming, particularly to Thatcher, was the return of inflation, that key foe that she thought she had trounced once and for all. Down to only 5 percent in 1987, it climbed to 8 percent in 1989 and all the way up to 11 percent by the autumn of 1990. Thatcher's Chancellors of the Exchequer—Geoffrey Howe, Nigel Lawson, and John Major—all argued that the solution to inflation lay in joining the exchange rate mechanism (ERM), a system established in 1979 by EC member states as a means of stabilizing international currency exchanges and preparing the way for a single European currency. Thatcher, however, regarded such a move as essentially a retreat, a backward step that would revive the exchange controls that she had abolished as soon as she took office. "There is no way to buck the market," she insisted.[29] Even more fundamentally,

Thatcher saw that the ERM was only a halfway house (as it was intended to be) toward a single European currency, which she dismissed as "some airy-fairy concept which in my view will never come in my lifetime."[30]

In the short term, at least, events proved Thatcher correct about the ERM, although not about the single currency (which entered circulation as the euro in eleven European states in 2002). By October, 1990, with inflation up to almost 11 percent, the consensus within Britain's political and financial communities was that Britain had to join the ERM. Thatcher, of course, had always insisted she was a conviction rather than a consensus politician and all her convictions were against joining the European monetary system. Yet she gave way, at what turned out to be the worst possible time. A few weeks after Britain joined the ERM and pegged the value of the pound to the German mark, East and West Germany united. The economic costs of German unification turned out to be far more than anyone had expected, and the mighty German economy sputtered to a halt. Just two years later, an international run on the pound forced the British government to pull out of the ERM.

But by then Thatcher had been forced out of office—and the issue that forced her out was "Europe," and more specifically, divisions between her and the rest of her government regarding the EC's plans for a common European currency. Throughout the autumn of 1990, officials in Thatcher's government had carefully and cautiously constructed a compromise policy that for a brief moment looked like it might reconcile all the various sides on this contentious issue. Caution, care, and compromise were never Thatcher's style, however, and in a raucous Commons debate on the issue, the prime minister unilaterally contradicted, and so destroyed, this effort at compromise.

This action drove Geoffrey Howe—former Chancellor of the Exchequer, former Foreign Secretary, and one of the most prominent men in government—to resign. Everyone, however, expected that this gentle, even meek man (and notoriously boring speaker) would go quietly. They were wrong. On November 13, Howe stood up in the House of Commons to deliver the customary resignation speech. What followed was, according to the unanimous verdict of political and parliamentary historians, "one of the parliamentary occasions of the century."[31] Speaking quietly, Howe proceeded to demolish his prime minister. He hammered away at what he regarded as her misguided economic policies, her authoritarian approach to government, and most effectively, her "nightmare image" of a Europe "teeming with ill-intentioned people scheming, in her words, to 'extinguish democracy' and dissolve our national identities.'" In Howe's view, Thatcher's Europhobia threatened Britain's national interests; the future lay in the European Union. Britain had come late to Europe and its economy had suffered: "We have paid heavily in the past for late starts and squandered opportunities in Europe. We dare not let that happen again."[32]

Howe's speech set in motion the parliamentary party processes that led to Thatcher's resignation. The day after his speech, a prominent Conservative announced his campaign for party leader. Thatcher had led her party to three colossal election victories. With a war against Iraq now looming, she could not believe that Conservative MPs would vote against her. Ignoring the advice of many of her supporters, she insisted on traveling to Paris for the international summit meeting to celebrate the end of the cold war. One of those supporters, the Conservative MP Alan Clark, recorded his despair in his diary: "The Party is virtually out of control. Mutinous . . . Code is abandoned. Discipline is breaking up." A few days later, Clark asked himself in disbelieving tones, "How can a narrow caucus in a singular political party unseat a Prime Minister just because it calculates that it may improve its election prospects thereby?"[33] But of course it could, and it did. In the first round of the leadership election, Thatcher won more votes than her challenger, but not the majority she needed to avoid a second ballot. The momentum for removing her then became unstoppable. Finally recognizing that she no longer had the support of her parliamentary party, Thatcher announced her intention of stepping down on November 22. The BBC pronounced it "an historic moment and the end of an era in British politics."[34] Meeting with her Cabinet , Thatcher mused, "It's a funny old world."[35] Six days later, she moved out of No. 10 Downing Street and delivered her resignation to the queen.

CHAPTER 8

| THE VICTORY OF THATCHERISM |

IN AN INTERVIEW shortly after she left office, Thatcher declared, "Thatcherism is not for a decade. It is for centuries."[1] The survival of any "ism" over centuries may be doubtful, but Thatcherism certainly did outlast Thatcher. The woman was pushed out of power in December 1990, but the revolution moved on. In Britain, subsequent governments, both Conservative and Labour, consolidated and extended the Thatcher revolution. Thatcher came into office promising to restore the "Great" in "Great Britain" and many observers believed she did so. Thatcherism transformed Britain into a much more economically vigorous society that once again stood at the very hub of global finance and that once again played an important role in world affairs. As the new century opened, talk of British decline seemed antiquated. Moreover, many of the ideas Thatcher first promoted in the 1970s crossed British borders and influenced political and social life throughout much of the world as part of the New Conservative revolution. Yet Thatcher did not succeed in all that she set out to do, and the legacy of Thatcherism remains sharply disputed.

Thatcher's removal from office in 1990 did not mean an election or a new party in power. Instead, Thatcher's chosen successor moved into No. 10 Downing Street. Although dramatically different from Thatcher in his personality and governing style, John Major not only continued but extended his predecessor's programs. At the age of forty-seven when he took office, Major was the youngest prime minister in the twentieth century (until his successor, Tony Blair, took over at age forty-three). Major had entered the House of Commons in 1979 and thus had never experienced political life except under Thatcher. Little known outside of parliament until 1989, he suddenly vaulted into prominence when Thatcher, to the surprise of many observers, appointed him Foreign Secretary and then Chancellor of the Exchequer. By all accounts a kind and decent man, Major was far less charismatic than his predecessor and also far less authoritarian. Many Britons both inside and outside of Westminster greeted his premiership with relief. After the turmoil of the Thatcher years, he seemed to promise quieter waters.

And yet under Major the Thatcher Revolution accelerated; even when Major did shift course, the overall direction remained the same. For example, he replaced the much-loathed poll tax with a "council tax" based on property ownership, but local governments were not allowed to set the level of their tax. Instead, the central state maintained control over funding and therefore over policy and priorities. Thus the centralizing, standardizing side of Thatcherism continued unabated. Major also consolidated Thatcherism's pro-business agenda not only by banning the closed shop, and thus stripping unions of one of their last bastions of power, but also by abolishing the Wages Councils that, ever since 1908, had set minimum wage rates in nonunionized sectors of the economy. Many of the more controversial of Thatcher's plans were actually implemented under Major, including the privatization of the electricity industry and the imposition of the National Curriculum on all schools.

Major also pushed privatization beyond what Thatcher herself had dared attempt. Despite the urgings of some of her more radical advisors, Thatcher had refused to privatize the coal industry—for so long the center of labor militancy—or the huge, somewhat antiquated, but functional and fundamentally necessary British railway system. Major, however, did not hesitate.

In 1994, the coal industry moved into the private sector after several years of preparation, which included the closure of many mines and the devastation of many mining communities. The Major government also privatized British Rail, a colossal and, almost everyone agrees, catastrophic endeavor that produced twenty-five different passenger lines, plus separate companies for the various services, stations, and even track. Mass chaos, and a series of horrific crashes, ensued but the railways remained in private hands.

Major's fiscal policies also echoed those of his mentor. When Major took office in 1990, inflation stood at 9 percent. To bring down the inflation rate, he and his chancellor Norman Lamont opted for the deflationary measures Thatcher had utilized to such effect a decade earlier: high interest rates and high unemployment numbers (back to 3 million by 1993) squeezed inflation out of the economy. By the middle of the decade, growth had returned and the unemployment rate, at 6.7 percent, was lower than in any other European country.[2] Here the impact of the Thatcher Revolution is clear: an unemployment rate of almost 7 percent would have been greeted as a tragedy at any time between 1950 and 1970; now it had been redefined as acceptable.

On May 1, 1997, the Conservative Party finally lost a general election, and did so dramatically: with 418 seats to the Conservatives' 165, the Labour Party held a decisive majority. The election, however, proved *not* to be a turning point. Rather than rejecting or reversing Thatcherism, the "New Labour" governments of Tony Blair and Gordon Brown consolidated the Thatcher Revolution. In many ways, Blair was even more a Thatcherite than Major, despite his party affiliation. Blair's approach to government, for example, more closely resembled Thatcher's. Major genuinely believed in Cabinet government and sought to develop consensus among Cabinet ministers for government policies. Blair, however, shared Thatcher's impatience with and even contempt for Cabinet government. He and a small set of unelected advisors made the important decisions without Cabinet input.

NEW LABOUR. *Together, Tony Blair and Gordon Brown remade the Labour Party to enable it to compete in a political climate transformed by Thatcher's New Conservatism.*

The youngest prime minister in Britain since 1812, Blair was only twenty-one years old when Thatcher took power in 1979. His adult life, therefore, had been spent in a Thatcherist political culture. As ambitious young MPs in the 1980s, Blair and his House of Commons officemate Gordon Brown set out to revamp the Labour Party so that it could win elections in this Thatcherist world. They recognized that "Old Labour's" traditional base, the unionized industrial working class, was disappearing and so they focused on severing the Labour Party from its union roots and appealing to the widening ranks of middle-class voters. According to Blair, "We play the Tory [Conservative] game when we speak up for the under-class rather than the broad majority of people in this country."[3] New Labour emphasized middle-class concerns such as security, law and order, and economic growth.

When Blair took office in 1997, one of the first people he invited to No. 10 Downing Street was Margaret Thatcher. This meeting symbolized Thatcher's ultimate victory. Blair proclaimed that Thatcher had got it right, that before Thatcher "there was too much collective power, too much bureaucracy, too much state intervention. . . . The era of corporatist state intervention is over."[4] Cabinet minister Peter Mandelson put it more clearly, "We are all Thatcherists now."[5] With Brown as Chancellor of the Exchequer, the New Labour government emphasized balanced budgets, low inflation, and a strong pound. By 1999, the United Kingdom was rated first out of the then twenty-two countries in the Organisation for Economic Co-Operation and Development (OECD) for "economic freedom" and "entrepreneurial welcome."

Blair's enthusiasm for privatization also revealed the essential Thatcherism of New Labour. When Blair first took office, many people expected that his government would reverse the highly unpopular and extremely expensive privatization of British Rail. After ten years in private hands, the various British railway companies now cost the Treasury (and hence the taxpayer) five times what they had under public ownership. Blair, however, not only refused to renationalize British Rail; he also continued to whittle away at what remained of the public sector by privatizing the air control system and proposing to privatize the London Underground (the Tube). In addition, those aspects of the economy and political life that remained under public control were now subject to market testing, on the assumption that the methods of private business were innately more efficient and rational than those of public service. What the influential British journalist Simon Jenkins has called the "culture of audit" flourished under Blair: everything that could be counted, was; if it couldn't be counted, it didn't count.[6]

Foreign affairs also illustrated the Thatcherist nature of both the Major and the Blair governments. In the decades after Thatcher stepped off the world stage, Britain's foreign policy continued to rest on three key Thatcherist assumptions: ambivalence toward the European Union, the primacy of the Atlantic relationship, and the efficacy of military intervention around the globe.

The continuity of policy did not, however, indicate the existence of a widely shared national consensus. In foreign affairs as in economic and social policy, Thatcherism produced controversy and division in Britain.

Thatcher's growing hostility toward the European Union (EU) led directly to her removal from power; this dramatic action did not, however, unite either the Conservative Party or the general public behind the European project. Instead, it initiated years of party and popular division over the EU. Although far more favorably disposed toward the EU than was Thatcher, Major found it impossible to lead Britain very far down the European path. Thatcher herself, once she was out of office, gave her Euroscepticism free rein, even at one point comparing the EU unfavorably with the Soviet Union: "A half-Europe imposed by Soviet tyranny is one thing; a half-Europe imposed by Brussels would be a moral catastrophe."[7] Faced with vociferous opposition to the idea of any loss of national sovereignty to the EU, Major largely continued along Thatcherist lines—although never closely enough to satisfy his one-time mentor. Much to Thatcher's horror, Major signed the Maastricht Treaty that created the EU in 1991, but he did so only after making it clear that Britain would not abide by the Social Charter nor opt for the single currency. "I will never, come hell or high water, let our distinctive British identity be lost in a federal Europe," Major promised.[8] Under Major's leadership, as under Thatcher, large sections of the Conservative Party and of the wider British public remained unconvinced of the virtues of British membership in the EU.

EU membership also remained a divisive issue under New Labour. The European question was at the heart of the growing divide between Blair and Brown, with the enthusiastic and cheerful Blair more instinctively pro-European than his dour chancellor. As the man in charge of the money, Brown insisted that Britain could not adopt the euro (the EU single currency) unless a series of rigorous criteria were met; in consequence, Britain stuck with the pound sterling despite Blair's initial pro-euro stance.

Blair's government did adopt the EU Social Charter (out of which Major had opted), but in keeping with New Labour's pro-business slant, failed to implement most of its provisions. Under New Labour as under Thatcher, Britain remained in but not of Europe, with much of the public and the political elite sharply at odds over the pace and position of Britain in the EU.

This continuing ambivalence toward Europe complemented the additional Thatcherist legacies of a strong Atlanticism and an interventionist foreign policy, both on display in the war that John Major inherited from Thatcher. Saddam Hussein's invasion of Kuwait—and the threat of an Iraqi seizure of Saudi oil fields—resulted in the formation of an Anglo-American-led coalition against Iraq in the late summer of 1990. When Thatcher left office at the end of the year, plans were well underway for the aerial bombardment that began on January 17, 1991 and the ground assault that began on February 24. The "boots on the ground" phase of the war lasted only four days. With Iraq driven back behind its borders, the coalition ceased military action. This limited and decisive engagement sent Major's poll numbers soaring and cemented his relationship with the American president George H. W. Bush. It also seemed to confirm Thatcher's belief in an activist foreign policy structured around close ties between the United States and Britain.

These trends grew even more pronounced under New Labour. As Thatcher did with Reagan and Major with George H. W. Bush, Tony Blair forged a close working relationship with US president Bill Clinton—and much like Thatcher did with Reagan, used this relationship to shape global policy and to foster an activist, interventionist approach. At Blair's urging, NATO forces deployed air strikes in Kosovo to halt Serbian nationalist efforts to "cleanse" the region of ethnic Albanians.

The success of this intervention helps explain Blair's unqualified support for the wars declared by US President George W. Bush after the terrorist attacks against the United States on September 11, 2001. Like Thatcher, Blair had come to conclude first, that Britain must provide unstinting support for its foremost ally and, second, that British and American troops could and must intervene where necessary to make the world a safer and more prosperous place. Unlike the Falklands War or the Gulf War of 1991, however, the Anglo-American invasion of Iraq in 2003 proved immensely controversial. Because the Iraqi government was not linked to the 9/11 attacks, many European governments opposed the invasion as did most of the British public. An antiwar demonstration in London in February 2003 attracted 1 million people, the largest public protest in British history. Blair, however, remained firm in his support for the venture, even after its initial justification—the Iraqi possession of weapons of mass destruction—turned out to be false. As so often under Thatcher, division and disagreement rather than consensus characterized British political culture in the wake of Blair's global activism. The enormous unpopularity of the Iraq war was the principal reason Blair was forced to cede his party's leadership, and the office of prime minister, to Gordon Brown in 2007.

The record of the Major and Blair governments shows that while Thatcher lost power in 1990, Thatcherism continued to flourish in Britain. Yet Thatcherism also encountered sharp limits. Polls showed that Britons more strongly favored welfare spending when Thatcher left office in 1990 than they had in 1979.[9] Even Thatcher herself had never been able to reduce social spending, nor was she able to convince the majority of British voters of the virtues of self-reliance and individualism over a broad safety net and collective provision. This widespread refusal to abandon the social democratic commitment to collective welfare was one of the most strikingly anti-Thatcherist aspects of the New Labour governments of Tony Blair and Gordon Brown. From 2002 on, Brown as Chancellor of the Exchequer loosened the controls on social spending in an effort to make up for the deterioration of services after two decades of Conservative government. The National Health Service, in particular, benefited from a massive infusion of funds. More generally, unlike Thatcher and contrary to Thatcherism, New Labour did not condemn income redistribution and social equality as inherently bad. Its policies sought to restore to British society a sense of collective responsibility and communal good, at the same time that it endeavored to retain the Thatcherist emphasis on individual achievement and economic entrepreneurship.

This commitment to collective welfare extended beyond post-Thatcher Britain. In no western European state was there a full-scale retreat from the postwar commitment to collective welfare, even as governments across the political spectrum adopted New Conservative fiscal and monetary policies. Most Europeans (and most Canadians, Australians, and New Zealanders) remained convinced of the economic necessity and moral value of the welfare states they had built in the wake of World War II. Even during and after the 1990s, polls showed that Europeans were willing to pay higher tax rates to fund state provision for collective welfare.[10]

Similarly, Thatcher's rejection of corporatism and her concurrent gutting of trade union power did not become universal. In the United States, New Conservatives such as Ronald Reagan did regard a politically powerful union movement as a block to economic growth and did embark on efforts to rein in union power through legislation and, in the case of an air traffic controllers' strike in 1981, a well-publicized showdown akin to Thatcher's fight with the miners. In the former communist states of Eastern Europe in the 1990s, the political climate was also antiunion because of the link between the now delegitimized communist regimes and the official unions they had sanctioned. But in western Europe and in Canada, antiunionism was far less potent and corporatism continued to serve as a basic pillar of many political structures. In Germany, for example, unions worked with the central government and with employers' organizations to meet the challenges of stagflation, reunification, and energy diversification without massive unemployment.

Although the welfare state and corporatism continued to characterize many Western societies, by the 1990s two core elements of Thatcherism—the rejection of Keynesianism and privatization—had become the economic orthodoxy and the central pillars of the New Conservatism. Thatcher had never been persuaded by the Keynesian argument that capitalist economies were inherently unstable and that the state needed to intervene in economic affairs and modulate the market in order to ensure full employment. In the 1950s and 1960s, with Western economies experiencing an unprecedented boom under Keynesian economic direction, Thatcher's adherence to liberal economics seemed nonsensical at best. The stagflation of the 1970s, however, transmuted the outlandish into the mainstream. Shaken by high inflation and negative growth rates, governments followed Thatcher's lead in emphasizing monetary control and market forces over fiscal management and, more broadly, in abandoning the postwar commitment to using the state's power to ensure full employment. In the 1980s and 1990s, Thatcher's rejection of Keynesian demand management went global as the International Monetary Fund and the World Bank imposed austerity regimes on states seeking economic aid.

The rejection of Keynesianism sounded the death knell for nationalized industries. The idea of public control, embraced in the 1950s and 1960s as a way to manage capitalist economies more effectively, came to seem an illusion. By the 1990s, privatization—a word that, ironically, Thatcher never liked—had become a kind of governing mantra, as governments from Australia and New Zealand to Latin America to the post-communist states of Eastern Europe shifted assets from public to private ownership.[11] Under just two years of the professedly Socialist government of Lionel Jospin (which took office in 1997), for example, France privatized more state property than it had during the administrations of Jospin's five predecessors.[12] All total, in the years between 1990 and 2000, European governments privatized over $420 billion worth of state assets in what has been described as "the greatest sale in the history of the world."[13]

Thatcherism was about more than economics, however. In Thatcher's view, the social democratic settlement had deprived Britain of its entrepreneurial spirit, weakened its global position, and sapped its moral strength. Thatcherism, therefore, was in many ways a movement of national restoration and revival, an effort to reverse what Thatcher perceived as over two decades of decline in not only economic indices but also international affairs and even social morality. Given the breathtaking scale of its ambition, it is hardly surprising that Thatcherism did not succeed in all it set out to do and that its legacy remains highly controversial.

Thatcherism failed most conspicuously in its efforts to retain and to strengthen traditional moral codes. Although liberal in its economics, Thatcherism did not embrace the idea of individual freedom in the moral realm. Disturbed by what she and other conservatives labeled the "permissive society," Thatcher sought to strengthen the traditional definitions of social morality that she and many of her supporters believed had long undergirded British society. She proved unable, however, to turn the clock back; the evolution (or as Thatcher would term it, the decline) of British social morality continued at a rapid pace during and after the Thatcher years. The rates of couples choosing to cohabit rather than marry, for example, increased steadily from Thatcher's accession to power in 1979 to the present day, while gay marriage ceremonies, both civil and religious, are now legal everywhere in the United Kingdom except Northern Ireland. Comparative statistics on a range of issues show how far the British have traveled from the sort of society for which Thatcher longed: Britain possesses one of the lowest church attendance rates in Europe, the highest divorce rate and the highest incidence of violent crime in the EU, the highest teenage pregnancy and abortion rates in western Europe, and the highest percentage of single mothers anywhere in Europe except Estonia. If judged

by its success in promoting what Thatcher often called "our traditional way of life," Thatcherism failed.

Thatcherism also failed in its effort to code "Britishness" to
mean the island's indigenous white and largely Christian population. Despite legislation banning further mass non-white immigration, Britain by the beginning of the twenty-first century had
become a multiracial society, with ethnic minorities comprising 7
percent of the total population. High cross-racial marriage rates and
a vibrant popular culture resulting from the fusion of different
ethnic and religious traditions point to the emergence of a successful multicultural society. After the London transit bombings of
July 7, 2005—which saw four British Islamist suicide bombers kill
almost 50 people and injure another 700—attention focused on the
alienation and anger of young British Muslims; the vast majority of
British Muslims, however, are proud to call themselves British.

A recent survey that showed 77 percent of British Muslims
"strongly identifying" with Britain also showed that only 50 percent of the wider population did so. [14] This latter figure highlights
another area in which Thatcher did not achieve quite what she
set out to do. Thatcher aimed to restore the "Great" to "Great
Britain"; ironically, her policies weakened the ties that bound
together the constituent British nations. Welsh and Scottish
nationalism long predated Thatcher's governments, but the
results of her policies strengthened the separatist arguments.
Throughout the Thatcher years, the disproportionate concentra-
tion of unemployment in these regions eroded ties to the London
government. More generally, by destroying the social democratic
consensus forged during World War II, Thatcher cut a central
strand of "Britishness." Protestant Christianity and a fear of continental powers (France in the eighteenth and nineteenth centuries,
Germany in the twentieth) had long woven a common sense of
British national identity, but in the post–World War II era these
threads became increasingly frayed. To a large degree, the war and
the political consensus that grew out of it took their place. The
memory of World War II as a time when all classes and

nationalities—English, Scottish, Welsh, Northern Irish—had pulled together and achieved something lasting, something good and decent and quintessentially British, helped hold together a sense of common British identity. As this conviction faded and the social democratic political culture fractured, the centrifugal forces of Welsh and Scottish separatism grew stronger. The New Labour government's effort to harness these forces through limited devolution resulted in the formation of a separate Welsh assembly and Scottish parliament in 1999. Scottish nationalism, however, has continued to gain in strength. A referendum for Scottish independence in September 2014 narrowly failed to pass and in the general elections the following spring, the Scottish Nationalist Party won 56 of the 59 Scottish seats in the House of Commons.

In 2006, British newspapers and commentators heralded the twentieth anniversary of the "Big Bang," the overnight deregulation and modernization of London's stock market that so transformed the British financial sector and so much represented Thatcherism's impact. With London as the dominant force in a booming global economy, celebration was the order of the day. Two years later, the world looked very different. A decade's worth of risky financial ventures, many of them linked to what at the time had seemed an ever-expanding housing market, ravaged the global economy. Credit dried up, businesses went under, and unemployment rose. On September 15, 2008, the American financial firm Lehman Brothers filed for bankruptcy, the largest such filing in global history. The next day, the overnight interbank lending rate (the interest charged on very short-term loans between banks) in London doubled. Within three weeks, Prime Minister Gordon Brown was forced to announce a £500 billion ($850 billion) bailout of British banks, in an effort to stop the entire British financial system from collapsing. Over the next few months, the United States and many European governments followed in Brown's footsteps as they struggled to respond to the worst global economic crisis since the Great Depression.

In the shadow of these events, the Big Bang appeared rather different to many commentators, less a cause of celebration than of crisis. Seeking to explain the events of 2008, many economists and other observers questioned whether Thatcherist deregulation had created a financial culture that sacrificed long-term prosperity for short-term profits. They argued that by dismantling the boundaries that had separated those who created stock options from those who advised customers on the purchase of such options, the Big Bang produced a system based on an inherent conflict of interest. As the personal tragedies piled up— homes lost, ambitions scuttled, savings depleted—politicians, policymakers, and ordinary people debated whether that Thatcherist faith in the free market was fully justified.

The debate, of course, continues. The causes of the crash of 2008 continue to be immensely controversial and its consequences lingered long. In Britain, the general election results of 2010 epitomized the confusion and division engendered by the economic crisis. Disgruntled voters turned away from Gordon Brown and New Labour in numbers large enough to ensure that for the first time in thirteen years, the party lost control of the House of Commons—but not large enough for an outright Conservative victory. The result was a "hung parliament" with the Conservative Party, led by David Cameron, forced to form a coalition with the Liberal Democrats.

The last such hung parliament was in 1974, in the midst of a decade marked by economic stagnation and political disarray, the period of multifaceted crisis that gave birth to Thatcherism. More than thirty-five years later, economic stagnation and political disarray once again characterized British society. And once again, a Conservative prime minister without a wide base of popular support promised to address those problems with dramatic measures. Faced with a crippling national debt, Cameron announced the largest cuts in public spending since World War II. The time had come, he insisted, to rid Britain of what remained of its social democratic legacy. Once again, huge numbers of protesters took

DAVID CAMERON AND MARGARET THATCHER AT 10 DOWNING STREET, 2010. *Twenty years after Thatcher left office, her ideas continued to shape British politics.*

to the streets to demonstrate their disapproval of the prime min-ister's policies.[15] Clearly Thatcherism, both its ideas and its legacy of division, remained a potent force in British society.

In addition, the economic crisis gave further impetus to the anti-EU forces within Britain that Thatcher had helped invigorate. As governments responded to the threat of financial breakdown with banking bailouts, levels of government debt rose, and in some European countries, reached catastrophic levels. At this point, the weakness of the single currency became clear: crises in Spain or Ireland had an immediate and direct impact on the economic and fiscal stability of the entire "Eurozone." Britain, of course, had yet to adopt the euro and, in the wake of what became known as the Eurozone debt crisis, looked much less likely to do so. The debt crisis also increased the numbers of Britons who questioned the value of British membership in the EU.[16] Cameron announced plans to hold a national referendum on Britain's EU membership, despite—or perhaps because of—the complete lack of consensus within his own party, let alone the country, on the issue.

Questions about the links between Thatcherist policies and the post-2008 economic crisis, the hung parliament of 2010, the increasingly hostile debate about Britain's place in the EU—all of these demonstrate how controversial Thatcher and Thatcherism remains in Britain today. The reactions to Thatcher's death both illustrated and accentuated that controversy. After a period of ill health, Margaret Thatcher died of a stroke on April 8, 2013. Cameron's Conservative government immediately began to put into effect longstanding plans for a grand, publicly funded funeral to be broadcast to the world. Tributes to Thatcher poured in from all over Britain and across the globe. The reaction of the senior Conservative MP David Davis was typical of many of Thatcher's supporters:

> Margaret Thatcher was the greatest of modern British prime ministers, and was central to the huge transformation of the whole world that took place after the fall of the Soviet Union. Millions of people in Britain and around the world owe her a debt of gratitude for their freedom and their quality of life, which was made possible by her courageous commitment to the principles of individual freedom and responsibility.[17]

At the same time, however, Thatcher Death Parties erupted in British streets, particularly in the economically depressed cities of northern England and Scotland and the coal-mining communities of Wales and the Midlands. Kicking into gear a plan first proposed in 2007, Thatcher's critics encouraged mass purchases of the song "Ding, Dong, the Witch Is Dead," in an effort to force the main popular music station in Britain, BBC Radio 1, to play the song on its weekly Top Ten countdown. The song reached no. 2. Faced with calls from Conservative MPs and others to ban the song, the BBC chose instead to play only a five-second excerpt.[18] The BBC's refusal to broadcast the song in its entirety mattered little as versions of it appeared all over social media, along with expressions of rage at and hostility toward Thatcher and all that she had stood for. Even in death, Thatcher remained a powerful and a divisive force.

PRIMARY SOURCE EXCERPTS AND STUDY QUESTIONS

THIS BOOK HAS EMPHASIZED TWO interconnecting themes: (1) Margaret Thatcher's efforts to break with the postwar political consensus and to construct a New Conservatism, and (2) the interplay between Thatcher's political ideology and her public image. As you examine the following excerpts from Thatcher's interviews and speeches, think about these themes.

I.

The first primary source excerpt comes from a Yorkshire Television interview that Thatcher gave to Dr. Miriam Stoppard in 1985 on a program called Woman to Woman. *Stoppard, a medical doctor, was also a well-known television personality who frequently anchored programs on medical and health topics.*

PRIME MINISTER: Well, home really was very small and we had no mod cons[a] and I remember having a dream that the one thing I really wanted was to live in a nice house, you know, a house with more things than we had.

DR. STOPPARD: When you say "no mod cons" what do you mean?

PRIME MINISTER: We had not got hot water. We only had a cold water tap. We had to heat all the hot water in a copper. There was

---

[a] "mod cons" = "modern conveniences."

an outside toilet. So when people tell me about these things, I know about them, but everything was absolutely clean, bright as a new pin and we were taught cleanliness was next to godliness, and yes, I often used to get down and polish the floor. We had lino[b] on the floor, because both the floor and the old-fashioned mahogany furniture had to be clean. It was absolutely imperative and yes, everything had to be washed and washed and washed again. And we did a bake twice a week. My mother was very busy. This is why I learned to be busy. And my father was very busy. We used every hour of every day. We used to bake twice a week, a big bake, twice a week.

DR. STOPPARD: What did you actually do when you baked?

PRIME MINISTER: Baking, you baked your own bread, you baked your own pastry, you did quite a lot of steam puddings, you would do quite a number of pies; you would always bottle fruit; you would do about twenty Christmas puddings just before Christmas and they would last you until Easter, you know, one or two a week. Oh yes, we had no such thing as a refrigerator. I only knew one person in our circle who had a refrigerator. We had no such thing as a vacuum cleaner—dustpan and brush all the time. No such things as sprays in those days, no hard polishing, but cleanliness was vital. Washday Monday, ironing Tuesday. Washday, no washing machine. Washed it in a great big dolly tub with a dolly[c] and a great big mangle[d] and then everything was very nicely mangled. A great big ironing day Tuesday, and so one was brought up really in a very regular way and my mother did all of that. She made our clothes. We would paint and redecorate our own rooms and she would work in the shop, and I was always used to being in and out of the shop, so that is where I got used to talking to almost anyone and everyone.

---

[b] "lino" = linoleum.
[c] "dolly" = large wooden forked paddle for stirring the dirty clothes in the tub.
[d] "mangle" = rollers for squeezing the water out of laundered clothes.

But I was used to my mother working hard and of course, she took over when my father went out to do voluntary things, and we did. We were very prominent in the church. We did things for the church; we did things for National Savings; we did things for what in those days was called the League of Pity . . . these days it is the NSPCC.[e] You were taught to take part. You were part of something and you were taught to take part. And whenever we did a bake, then we always took out either a few loaves or some home-made cakes for someone who was not well. That was just part of doing the ordinary bake.

DR. STOPPARD: Can you tell me a little bit about your father?

PRIME MINISTER: My father left school when he was 13 . . . 12, 13 . . . he really was very bright. In these days, he would gone to university, but in those days there weren't the opportunities and he went to work in a local grocer's shop. And . . . I remember him telling me he earned 14 shillings a week and 12 shillings went to digs,[f] the cost of digs; the next priority was one shilling to be saved, and then you spent the next shilling. But note, one shilling had to be saved. You did not save what you have got left; there was a priority to save.[1]

II.

The second excerpt comes from a speech that Thatcher delivered in New York City shortly after she became Leader of the Conservative Party. It was widely applauded in the United States and marked the beginning of Thatcher's continuing American popularity.

---

[e] National Society for the Prevention of Cruelty to Children

[f] "digs" = housing.

1. TV Interview for Yorkshire Television Woman to Woman, October 2, 1985/Thatcher Archive: COI transcript; MTF: http://margaretthatcher.org/document/105830; accessed 12/30/2012

Only a week or two ago, Vermont Royster[g] wrote that—and I quote—"Britain today offers a textbook case on how to ruin a country." I do take some consolation that there's only one small vowel sound between 'ruin' and 'run' a country. The small vowel sound is 'I'. [Laughter and applause] However, the rather fatalistic tone of much of what is written about Britain by commentators on both sides of the Atlantic is, I believe, misplaced. . . .

I think most outside observers have noticed that, amid our very well published difficulties, a new debate is beginning . . . about the proper role of government, the Welfare State, and the attitudes on which both rest. And may I stress that the attitudes are extremely important? Of course, many of the issues at stake have been debated on countless occasions in the last century or two and some are as old as philosophy itself, but the Welfare State in Britain is now at least thirty years old. So, after a long period in which it was unquestionably accepted by the whole of society, we can now do more than discuss its strengths and weaknesses in the abstract language of moral and political principles. We can depart from theory and we can actually look at the evidence and see how it has worked, what effect it has had on the economy, how we ought now to assess it, before we decide what to go on and do next. The debate centres on what I'll term, for want of a better phrase, the "progressive consensus". . . . the doctrine that the state should be active on many fronts: in promoting equality, in the provision of social welfare, and in the redistribution of wealth and incomes. . . . [T]hese views have been held in varying degrees by all political parties, in schools and universities, and among social commentators generally. It's interesting that they're now being questioned right across the same broad spectrum. . . .

[T]he facts about economic inequality in Britain are these: that the rich are getting poorer and the poor have so far got richer. It's due both to market forces and the actions of government through the tax system. But if you look at the scope for further

---

[g] Editor of the *Wall Street Journal*.

redistribution now, there's very little left, because it's no longer the case that taking further money from the rich will make a significant difference to the wealth of the bulk of the population. We've come to the end of that road. . . .

The promotion of greater equality, of course, goes hand-in-hand with the extension of the Welfare State and state control over people's lives. Universal and usually 'free'—in inverted commas—social services necessarily transfer benefits in cash and kind from the richer to the poorer members of the community. . . . Now, how far has that process strengthened the economy? Because, if it hasn't strengthened the economy, you haven't the means to carry on, let alone improve your welfare. And one of the lessons we are learning in Britain is that you must, first of all, have the creation of wealth before you can put so much attention on to its distribution. . . .

Let me take a typical earner: a man and wife with two children on average industrial earnings. . . . In 1963, he used to pay in taxation, direct taxation, 5 percent of those average earnings to the state. Now, he pays 25 percent to the state. And, of course, you can imagine what's happened. He's said, "Well, I want to keep my net taxed income intact." And therefore it has been quite a strong factor in his demanding more wages and salaries to replace what in effect has been taken away in tax. . . . [T]his has led to a relentless acceleration of cost and price increases since that time, since the mid-1950s, when it was 2 percent per annum rate of inflation, to now when . . . it's 25 percent. . . .

[W]hat you find is, that people want to spend their own money to buy what they want when they want it. And they do not regard the substitution of state provided services as equivalent to spending their own money and in their own way. In a curious way, the attitudes in calling some things 'free' has led to the belief that the state services are really an absolute right and a kind of manna from heaven. Now, we've come to the end of that time. They're not manna from heaven. Government expenditure is private taxation or borrowing for which the citizen has to pay. . . .

Now, can you see where the cycle's got us to? Taking too much into public expenditure has meant trying to raise extra taxes. People have rebelled against that. They therefore have demanded extra wages. The companies have suffered, because we've had to have a certain amount of wage control, with price control, with profit control, so that companies have suffered also from extra taxes, also from loss of profits....

Now, all of these in fact have been the economic effects of pursuing far too much equality, and I think we have very much now come to the end of the road. And, in fact, we find that the persistent expansion of the role of the state, beyond the capacity of the economy to support it, and the relentless pursuit of equality has caused, and is causing, damage to our economy in a variety of ways. It's not the sole cause of what some have termed the 'British sickness' but it is a major one.

Now, what are the lessons then that we've learned from the last thirty years? First, that the pursuit of equality itself is a mirage. What's more desirable and more practicable than the pursuit of equality is the pursuit of equality of opportunity. And opportunity means nothing unless it includes the right to be unequal and the freedom to be different. One of the reasons that we value individuals is not because they're all the same, but because they're all different. I believe you have a saying in the Middle West: "Don't cut down the tall poppies. Let them rather grow tall." I would say, let our children grow tall and some taller than others if they have the ability in them to do so. Because we must build a society in which each citizen can develop his full potential, both for his own benefit and for the community as a whole, a society in which originality, skill, energy and thrift are rewarded, in which we encourage rather than restrict the variety and richness of human nature.... [2]

2. Speech to the Institute of SocioEconomic Studies ("Let Our Children Grow Tall"), September 15, 1975/ BBC Sound Archive, OUP transcript; MTF: http://margaretthatcher.org/document/102769; accessed 12/30/2012

III.

At the beginning of 1976, Thatcher jumped from the national to the world stage with what became known as the "Iron Lady" speech (see Chapter 4), in which she challenged the prevailing practice of détente between the West and the Soviet bloc and called for a much harder line in the cold war.

. . . . The Russians are bent on world dominance, and they are rapidly acquiring the means to become the most powerful imperial nation the world has seen. The men in the Soviet politburo don't have to worry about the ebb and flow of public opinion. They put guns before butter, while we put just about everything before guns. They know that they are a super power in only one sense— the military sense. They are a failure in human and economic terms. But let us make no mistake. The Russians calculate that their military strength will more than make up for their economic and social weakness. They are determined to use it in order to get what they want from us. . . . We must remember that there are no Queensbury rules[h] in the contest that is now going on. And the Russians are playing to win. . . .

The advance of Communist power threatens our whole way of life. That advance is not irreversible, providing that we take the necessary measures now. But the longer that we go on running down our means of survival, the harder it will be to catch up. In other words: the longer Labour remains in Government, the more vulnerable this country will be. (Applause.) . . . On defence, we are now spending less per head of the population than any of our major allies. . . . Of course, we are poorer than most of our NATO allies. This is part of the disastrous economic legacy of Socialism. But let us be clear about one thing. This is not a moment when anyone with the interests of this country at heart

---

[h] The code of rules in modern boxing, so called because John Douglas, 9th Marquess of Queensbury, endorsed the code in 1867.

should be talking about cutting our defences. It is a time when we urgently need to strengthen our defences. . . .

Throughout our history, we have carried the torch for freedom. Now, as I travel the world, I find people asking again and again, "What has happened to Britain?" They want to know why we are hiding our heads in the sand, why with all our experience, we are not giving a lead.

. . . . In the Conservative Party we believe that our foreign policy should continue to be based on a close understanding with our traditional ally, America. This is part of our Anglo-Saxon tradition as well as part of our NATO commitment, and it adds to our contribution to the European Community. Our Anglo-Saxon heritage embraces the countries of the Old Commonwealth that have too often been neglected by politicians in this country, but are always close to the hearts of British people. We believe that we should build on our traditional bonds with Australia, New Zealand and Canada, as well as on our new ties with Europe. . . . We stand with that select body of nations that believe in democracy and social and economic freedom.

Part of Britain's world role should be to provide, through its spokesmen, a reasoned and vigorous defence of the Western concept of rights and liberties . . . But our role reaches beyond this. We have abundant experience and expertise in this country in the art of diplomacy in its broadest sense. . . . The message of the Conservative Party is that Britain has an important role to play on the world stage. It is based on the remarkable qualities of the British people. Labour has neglected that role. . . . We are often told how this country that once ruled a quarter of the world is today just a group of offshore islands. Well, we in the Conservative Party believe that Britain is still great.

The decline of our relative power in the world was partly inevitable—with the rise of the super powers with their vast reserves of manpower and resources. But it was partly avoidable too—the result of our economic decline accelerated by Socialism. We must reverse that decline when we are returned to

Government. In the meantime, the Conservative Party has the vital task of shaking the British public out of a long sleep. Sedatives have been prescribed by people, in and out of Government, telling us that there is no external threat to Britain, that all is sweetness and light in Moscow, and that a squadron of fighter planes or a company of marine commandos is less important than some new subsidy. The Conservative Party must now sound the warning. There are moments in our history when we have to make a fundamental choice. This is one such moment—a moment when our choice will determine the life or death of our kind of society,—and the future of our children. Let's ensure that our children will have cause to rejoice that we did not forsake their freedom.[3]

IV.

The final primary source excerpt comes from Mrs. Thatcher's speech to the Conservative Party Conference in 1985. Every year Britain's political parties hold a conference at which they lay out their plans, policies, and principles; rally the faithful; and showcase up-and-coming political stars. Because many of the conference proceedings are televised, the annual party conference speech provides an important opportunity for the prime minister to reach not only the party rank-and-file but also the broader public.

Do you remember the Labour Britain of 1979? It was a Britain—in which union leaders held their members and our country to ransom;—A Britain that still went to international conferences

3. Speech at Kensington Town Hall ("Britain Awake") (The Iron Lady), January 19, 1976/Thatcher Archive, speaking text; MTF: http://www.margaretthatcher.org/document/102939; accessed 12/30/2012

but was no longer taken seriously;—A Britain that was known as the sick man of Europe;—And which spoke the language of compassion but which suffered the winter of discontent.

Governments had failed to tackle the real problems which afflicted us. They dodged difficult problems rather than face up to them. The question they asked was not "Will the medicine work?" But "Will it taste all right?"*[laughter]*

When we Conservatives said—"This is the way" they said—"forget it".

We were told you can't reform trade union leaders, you can't reform the trade unions—their leaders won't let you. But we did.

We were told you can't abolish price and wage controls—inflation will go up. But we did—and it came down.

We were told you can't give council tenants the right to buy. But we did—and the houses sold like hot cakes. *[applause]*

They said you can't denationalise—the unions won't wear it. But we did—and the workforce positively snapped up the shares. *[applause]*

And we were told you'll never stand a major industrial strike, let alone a coal strike. Mr. President, it lasted a whole year. But we did just that—and won. *[applause]* . . . And the nation stood with us; and a major strike, called without a ballot of its members, failed. It was a notable victory for a free, law-abiding people and their freely-elected democratic government. *[applause]*[4]

4. Speech to Conservative Party Conference, October 11, 1985/Thatcher Archive, speaking text; MTF: http://margaretthatcher.org/document/106145; accessed 12/30/2012

STUDY QUESTIONS

1. What was the "postwar political consensus"? What factors created it? What conditions sustained it?

2. When and why did the postwar political consensus break down? If Margaret Thatcher had decided after the birth of her twins to forego a political career, would this breakdown have occurred anyway?

3. Who would have been the likely audience for Stoppard's television interview with Thatcher (Excerpt I)? What message was Thatcher trying to convey? Did she succeed? How accurate was the picture that she painted of her childhood?

4. How important was Thatcher's childhood in shaping Thatcherism? How important was it that Thatcher was "Margaret" and not "Michael" or "Martin"?

5. In what ways did Thatcher's narrative in Excerpt I reflect and reinforce the ideas she presented in her speech in New York City in 1975 (Excerpt II)? Did it matter that Thatcher delivered this speech to an American audience? If so, how and why?

6. Excerpt II comes from what is often called Thatcher's "Let Our Children Grow Tall" speech. How does the idea of "Let Our Children Grow Tall" encapsulate many of the central ideas of Thatcherism? How might a social democrat respond to this speech?

7. Excerpt III is taken from one of Thatcher's most famous speeches on foreign affairs—and yet it is also very much a speech about British domestic politics. How so? In what ways does this speech demonstrate that Thatcher "tended to view her struggle against the social democratic consensus at home as part and parcel of the wider Western battle against global communism" (p. 79)?

8. Contrast the style of Thatcher's speech to the Conservative Party at its annual conference (Excerpt IV) with that of the two other speeches excerpted here. How can you account for the differences?

9. How does Excerpt IV help us understand the power and appeal of Thatcherism? How does it help us understand the weaknesses and limits of Thatcherism?

FURTHER READING

RECOMMENDED PRIMARY SOURCES

The essential primary source for any study of Margaret Thatcher is the Margaret Thatcher Foundation website: www.margaret-thatcher.org. This unbelievably rich and easy-to-use site contains the full texts of thousands of Thatcher's speeches, as well as video and audio clips, chronologies, commentaries, and interviews.

Additional recommended primary sources include the following:

Thatcher, Carol. *A Swim-On Part in the Goldfish Bowl: A Memoir.* London: Headline Review, 2008. Somewhat more superficial than Carol Thatcher's biography of her father (see below), but a useful look into Thatcher's family life.

Thatcher, Margaret. *The Downing Street Years* and *The Path to Power.* London: HarperCollins, 1993, 1995. Thatcher's two-volume memoir is of course an invaluable resource, although it must be used with care. Like most political autobiography, the story it tells is partial at best.

RECOMMENDED SECONDARY SOURCES

Campbell, John. *Margaret Thatcher, Vol. 1: The Grocer's Daughter* and *Vol. 2: The Iron Lady.* London: Pimlico, 2001, 2004. Campbell's biography stands as a central resource for any student of Margaret Thatcher. It is also available in an abridged edition: John Campbell, *Margaret Thatcher: From Grocer's Daughter to Iron Lady* (London: Vintage Books, 2009).

Moore, Charles. *Margaret Thatcher: The Authorized Biography. From Grantham to the Falklands.* New York: Alfred A. Knopf, 2013. Moore's biography appeared in print after I submitted the manuscript for *Margaret Thatcher: Shaping the New Conservatism,* and thus I was unable to make use of his work. No doubt, however, it will be a central source for Thatcher scholars.

Additional recommended secondary sources include the following:

Ball, Stuart and Anthony Seldon, eds. *The Heath Government 1970–1974.* London: Longman, 1996. A collection of essays that explore the various themes of the Heath years that so shaped Thatcher and Thatcherism.

Beckett, Andy. *When the Lights Went Out: What Really Happened to Britain in the Seventies.* London: Faber and Faber, 2009. A wonderfully written account that reads like a novel but rests on thorough research.

Evans, Eric. *Thatcher and Thatcherism.* London: Routledge, 1997. Part of Routledge's "Making of the Contemporary World" series, this short study provides both a chronological and thematic overview.

Foley, Michael. *The British Presidency.* Manchester, England: Manchester University Press, 2001. Foley uses Tony Blair's premiership to exemplify the contemporary trend toward leader-centered parties.

Green, E. H. H. *Thatcher.* London: Hodder Arnold, 2006. A thematic examination of Thatcher's politics and policies. Students new to British politics may find it relatively difficult.

Hanley, Lynsey. *Estates: An Intimate History.* London: Granta, 2007. A fascinating combination of history and autobiography and a compelling critique of Thatcherist housing reforms.

Harrison, Brian. *Seeking a Role: The United Kingdom 1961–1970* and *Finding a Role: The United Kingdom 1970–1990.* Oxford: Oxford University Press, 2009, 2010. Important studies of British foreign policy during the decades of Thatcher's political career.

Huber, Evelyn and John D. Stephens. *Development and Crisis of the Welfare State: Parties and Policies in Global Markets.* Chicago: University of Chicago Press, 2001. This important survey of postwar welfare states emphasizes the differences between the various policies and programs put in place after World War II.

Jenkins, Simon. *Thatcher & Sons: A Revolution in Three Acts*. London: Penguin, 2007. Jenkins, former editor of the *Times* (London) offers a lively, at times impassioned critique of the Thatcher Revolution.

Kavanagh, Dennis. *Thatcherism and British Politics: The End of Consensus?* Oxford: Oxford University Press, 1990. Although written very early (the first edition came out in 1987), this is a very important work for students. As the title indicates, Kavanagh places Thatcherism within the context of the breakdown of the postwar political consensus.

McLeod, Hugh. *The Religious Crisis of the 1960s*. Oxford: Oxford University Press, 2007. A superb examination of the context in which the "permissive society" emerged.

Nunn, Heather. *Thatcher, Politics and Fantasy: The Political Culture of Gender and Nation*. London: Lawrence and Wishart, 2002. A thought-provoking analysis of the gendering of Thatcher and Thatcherism.

Paul, Kathleen. *Whitewashing Britain: Race and Citizenship in the Postwar Era*. New York: Cornell University Press, 1997. Illuminating study of the response of British political leaders to the mass immigration of non-whites.

Reitan, Earl A. *The Thatcher Revolution: Margaret Thatcher, John Major, Tony Blair and the Transformation of Modern Britain, 1979–2001*. Lanham, MD: Rowman and Littlefield, 2003. Written with a North American audience in mind, this short survey provides an invaluable overview.

Sandbrook, Dominic. *Never Had It So Good: A History of Britain from Suez to the Beatles* and *White Heat: A History of Britain in the Swinging Sixties*. London: Little, Brown, 2005, 2006. Lengthy but lively popular histories provide a solid background for Thatcher's early career.

Sandbrook, Dominic. *The Way We Were: Britain, 1970–1974*. London: Penguin, 2010. Sandbrook continues his popular history of Britain; a good background to the Heath years.

Sandbrook, Dominic. *Seasons in the Sun: The Battle for Britain 1974–1979*. London: Allen Lane, 2012. Solid background to the years when Thatcherism was taking shape.

Seldon, Anthony (ed.). *Blair's Britain 1997–2007*. Cambridge: Cambridge University Press, 2007. A series of thematic essays written not only by historians and political scientists, but by a broad range of commentators and observers.

Seldon, Anthony and Daniel Collings. *Britain Under Thatcher*. London: Longman, 2000. Part of Longman's "Seminar Studies in History" series, this short book provides a valuable introduction.

Seldon, Anthony. *Major: A Political Life*. London: Orion Publishing, 1999. The scholarly biography of Thatcher's successor and protégé.

Taylor, Robert. *Major (British Prime Ministers of the Twentieth Century)*. London: Haus Publishing, 2006. Part of Haus' "Life and Times" series, this short book provides a good introduction to the Major years.

Thatcher, Carol. *Below the Parapet: A Biography of Denis Thatcher*. London: HarperCollins, 1997. Provides a poignant and honest glimpse of Thatcher's private life.

Timmins, Nicholas. *The Five Giants: A Biography of the Welfare State*. London: HarperCollins, 2001. A surprisingly good read; Timmins does a superb job of guiding the reader through what could have been dry-as-dust policy debates and highlighting the compelling human story.

Vinen, Richard. *Thatcher's Britain: The Politics and Social Upheaval of the Thatcher Era*. London: Simon and Schuster, 2009. Vinen disagrees with the interpretation offered in this book and argues that in many ways Thatcher defended the political consensus of the 1950s against what he labels the progressive consensus of the 1960s.

Yergin, Daniel and Joseph Stanislaw, *The Commanding Heights: The Battle for the World Economy*. New York: Free Press, 2002. Somewhat sensationalistic and oversimplified, but a good overview of triumph of New Conservative economics.

NOTES

CHAPTER 2

1. Quoted in John Campbell, *Margaret Thatcher, Vol. 1. The Grocer's Daughter* (London: Pimlico, 2001), p. 4.
2. Margaret Thatcher, *The Path to Power* (London: HarperCollins, 1995), p. 566.
3. Patricia Murray, *Margaret Thatcher* (London: W. H. Allen, 1980), p. 22.
4. Ibid., p. 13.
5. *Grantham Journal*, October 9, 1937; quoted in Campbell *Thatcher, Vol. 1*, p. 12.
6. October 2, 1985; TV Interview for Yorkshire Television *Woman to Woman* [Interviewer: Dr. Miriam Stoppard], No. 10 Downing Street. Source: Thatcher Archive: COI transcript; MTF: http://margaretthatcher.org/document/105830; accessed December 30, 2012.
7. Quoted in Campbell, *Thatcher, Vol. 1*, p. 24.
8. To Godfrey Winn, *Daily Express*, April 17, 1961; quoted in Campbell, *Thatcher, Vol. 1*, p. 19.
9. Quoted in Campbell, *Thatcher, Vol. 1*, p. 25.
10. Thatcher, *Path to Power*, p. 23.
11. Neville Chamberlain, *In Search of Peace* (New York: Putnam, 1939), p. 393.
12. Alfred Roberts's Rotary speech of January 1939, quoted in Campbell, *Thatcher, Vol. 1*, p. 39. For the church bells, see Andrew Chandler, "Munich and Morality: The Bishops of the Church of England and Appeasement," *Twentieth-Century British History*, 5, no. 1 (1994): 77–99.
13. Charles Ritchie, in Robert Mackay, *The Test of War: Inside Britain 1939–1945* (London: Routledge, 1999), p. 172.
14. Thatcher, *Path to Power*, pp. 37–38.
15. Campbell, *Thatcher, Vol. 1*, p. 45.
16. Ibid., p. 57.
17. Thatcher, *Path to Power*, p. 31.
18. Ibid., p. 46.
19. Ibid, p. 52, p. 69, p. 31.
20. Quoted in Margaret Jones and Rodney Lowe, *From Beveridge to Blair: The First Fifty Years of Britain's Welfare State, 1948–1998* (Manchester: Manchester University Press, 2002), p. 5.
21. Quoted in Campbell, *Thatcher, Vol. 1*, p. 50.
22. Thatcher, *Path to Power*, p. 566.

CHAPTER 3

1. John Campbell, *Margaret Thatcher: The Grocer's Daughter, Vol. 1* (London: Pimlico, 2001), p. 71.
2. Ibid., p. 73.
3. Ibid., p. 96.
4. Dominic Sandbrook, *White Heat: A History of Britain in the Swinging Sixties* (London: Abacus, 2006), p. 68.
5. Margaret Thatcher, *The Path to Power* (London: HarperCollins, 1995), p. 77.
6. Ibid., p. 63.
7. Monica Dickens, in *Woman's Own*, quoted in Sandbrook, *White Heat*, p. 695.
8. Quoted in E. H. H. Green, *Thatcher* (London: Bloomsbury Academic, 2006), p. 13.
9. Quoted in Campbell, *Thatcher, Vol. 1*, p. 121.
10. Ibid., p. 123.
11. Thatcher, *Path to Power*, p. 284.
12. *Evening News* (London), February 25, 1960; quoted in Campbell, *Thatcher, Vol. 1*, p. 124.
13. *Erith Observer*, April 8, 1949; quoted in Campbell, *Thatcher, Vol. 1*, p. 77.
14. *Kentish Independent*, September 23, 1949; quoted in Campbell, *Thatcher, Vol. 1*, p. 78.
15. April 1954; quoted in Green, p. 14.
16. *Evening News* (London), October 5, 1959; quoted in Campbell, *Thatcher, Vol. 1*, p. 101.
17. Thatcher, *Path to Power*, p. 103.
18. Carol Thatcher, *Below the Parapet: The Biography of Denis Thatcher* (London: HarperCollins, 1997), p. 88.
19. Quoted in Hugo Young, *One of Us: A Biography of Margaret Thatcher* (London: Pan Books, 1989), p. 47.
20. Quoted in Campbell, *Thatcher, Vol. 1*, p. 144.
21. Ibid., p. 159.
22. Thatcher, *Path to Power*, p. 144.
23. Ivan Rowan, *Sunday Telegraph*, October 26, 1969; quoted in Campbell, *Thatcher, Vol. 1*, p. 194.
24. *The Right Road for Britain* (London: Conservative and Unionist Central Office, 1949).
25. *One Nation: A Tory Approach to Social Problems* (London: Conservative Political Centre, 1950), p. 16.
26. Quoted in T. W. Heyck and Meredith Veldman, *The Peoples of the British Isles. Volume III. From 1870 to the Present* (Chicago: Lyceum, 2014), p. 306.
27. Quoted in Campbell, *Thatcher, Vol. 1*, p. 78, p. 80.
28. Jim Prior, *A Balance of Power* (London: Hamish Hamilton, 1986), p. 53.

29. Campbell, *Thatcher, Vol. 1*, p. 179.
30. Thatcher, *Path to Power*, p. 263.
31. Margaret Thatcher, *The Downing Street Years* (London: HarperCollins, 1993), p. 663.
32. Quoted in John Hargreaves, *Decolonization in Africa* (London: Routledge, 1996), p. 113.
33. Sandbrook, *White Heat*, p. xvii.
34. Ibid., p. 492.
35. Ibid., p. 337.
36. Dominic Sandbrook, *State of Emergency: The Way We Were, Britain 1970–1974* (London: Penguin, 2011), p. 286.
37. Thatcher, *Path to Power*, p. 153.
38. Ibid., p. 152.
39. Quoted in Campbell, *Thatcher, Vol. 1*, p. 135.
40. Gordon Hawkins and Richard S. Frase, "Corporal Punishment," *Encyclopedia of Crime and Justice* (2002); http://www.encyclopedia.com/topic/corporal_punishment.aspx; accessed December 6, 2012.
41. Television interview on *A Plus 4* (Channel 4), October 15, 1984; MTF: http://www.margaretthatcher.org/speeches/displaydocument.asp?docid=105764; accessed December 6, 2012.

CHAPTER 4

1. The newspaper was the *Sun*, later one of Thatcher's most vigorous supporters. Quoted in E. H. H. Green, *Thatcher* (London: Bloomsbury Academic, 2006), p. 2.
2. Quoted in Simon Jenkins, *Accountable to None: The Tory Nationalization of Britain* (London: Penguin, 1995), p. 7.
3. Quoted in John Campbell, *Edward Heath: A Biography* (London: Jonathan Cape, 1993), p. 310.
4. Margaret Thatcher, *The Path to Power* (London: HarperCollins, 1995), p. 297.
5. Bernard Donoughue, *Downing Street Diary: With Harold Wilson in No. 10* (London: Pimlico, 2006), p. 503.
6. Quoted in Francis Wheen, *Strange Days Indeed: The 1970s: The Golden Age of Paranoia* (New York: PublicAffairs, 2010), pp. 250–251.
7. Quoted in J. Robert Wegs and Robert Landrech, *Europe Since 1945: A Concise History* (New York: Bedford St. Martin's, 1996), pp. 364–365.
8. Nicholas Timmins, *The Five Giants: A Biography of the Welfare* State (London: HarperCollins, 2001), p. 307.
9. House of Commons, November 17, 1965 (vol. 720, col. 1165). The American economist Paul Samuelson is frequently but incorrectly given the credit for coining the word "stagflation." See Edward Nelson and Kalin Nikolov, "Monetary Policy and Stagflation in the UK," Bank of England Working Paper Series, 2002, p. 9; http://www.bankofengland.co.uk/publications/Documents/workingpapers/wp155.pdf (accessed August 31, 2012).

10. Quoted in John Campbell, *Thatcher, Vol. 1, The Grocer's Daughter* (London: Pimlico, 2001), p. 281.

11. The headline is from the *Sunday Daily Express*; quoted in Thatcher, *Path to Power*, p. 188.

12. Headline in the *Sun*; quoted in Green, *Thatcher*, p. 2.

13. *Daily Mirror*, February 3, 1975; quoted in Campbell, *Thatcher, Vol. 1*, p. 296.

14. Barbara Castle, *The Castle Diaries, 1974–76* (London: Weidenfeld and Nicolson, 1980), p. 33.

15. Peter Clarke, "The Rise and Fall of Thatcherism," *Historical Research*, 72, no. 179 (October 1999): 301–322; p. 306.

16. Thatcher, *Path to Power*, p. 194.

17. Quoted in Patrick Cosgrave, *Margaret Thatcher: A Tory and Her Party* (London: Hutchinsonx, 1978), p. 14.

18. Speech to Finchley Conservatives, August 14, 1961, Margaret Thatcher Foundation. http://www.margaretthatcher.org/document/101105 (accessed December 18, 2012).

19. http://www.telegraph.co.uk/comment/3643823/Enoch-Powells-Rivers-of-Blood-speech.html (accessed August 9, 2012).

20. Amy Whipple, "Revisiting the 'Rivers of Blood' Controversy: Letters to Enoch Powell," *Journal of British Studies* 48 (July 2009): 717–735; Simon Heffer, *Like the Roman: The Life of Enoch Powell* (London: Faber and Faber, 1998), pp. 460–468.

21. Thatcher, *Path to Power*, p. 146.

22. *World in Action* [television interview], Jan 1978; see Thatcher, *Path to Power*, pp. 405–409; Campbell, *Thatcher, Vol. 1*, pp. 399–400; Alwyn Turner, *Crisis? What Crisis? Britain in the 1970s* (London: Aurum Press, 2008), p. 224.

23. Quoted in Campbell, *Thatcher, Vol. 1*, p. 383.

24. Speech at Kensington Town Hall, January 16, 1976; Margaret Thatcher Foundation: http://www.margaretthatcher.org/document/102939 (accessed December 16, 2012).

25. Speech to the Finchley Conservatives, January 31, 1976; Margaret Thatcher Foundation: http://www.margaretthatcher.org/document/102947 (accessed January 8, 2013).

26. House of Commons, June 9, 1976 (Vol. 912, cols. 1446–1457).

27. Speech to the Junior Carlton Club Political Council, May 4, 1976; Margaret Thatcher Foundation: http://www.margaretthatcher.org/document/103017 (accessed December 18, 2012).

28. Speech to Conservative Party Conference, October 8, 1976; Margaret Thatcher Foundation: http://www.margaretthatcher.org/document/103105 (accessed December 18, 2012).

29. Speech to Conservative Party Conference, October 10, 1980; Margaret Thatcher Foundation: http://www.margaretthatcher.org/document/104431 (accessed October 4, 2012).

30. Thatcher interview, *Early Evening News*, ITN, February 11, 1975; Margaret Thatcher Foundation: http://www.margaretthatcher.org/document/102618 (accessed January 8, 2013).

31. Conservative Economic Reconstruction Group meeting, July 5, 1975; quoted in Green, *Thatcher*, p. 69.

32. Alfred Sherman to Keith Joseph; quoted in Clarke, "Rise and Fall", p. 303.

33. Quoted in Timmins, *Five Giants*, p. 355.

34. Thatcher, *Path to Power*, p. 567.

35. Speech to the Zurich Economic Society, March 14, 1977; Margaret Thatcher Foundation: http://www.margaretthatcher.org/document/103336 (accessed December 18, 2012).

36. Speech, St. Lawrence Jewry, March 30, 1978; Margaret Thatcher Foundation: http://www.margaretthatcher.org/document/103522 (accessed December 18, 2012).

37. Speech to the Institute of Socio-Economic Studies, New York, September 15, 1975; Margaret Thatcher Foundation: http://www.margaretthatcher.org/document/102769 (accessed December 18, 2012).

38. Quoted in Turner, *Crisis?*, pp. 187–188.

39. Hughie Green on *Opportunity Knocks*; quoted in Turner, *Crisis?*, p. 189.

40. Quoted in Campbell, *Thatcher, Vol. 1*, p. 361.

41. Speech to the Conservative Party Conference, October 8, 1976.

42. John Hoskyns and Norman Strauss, *Stepping Stones* (Conservative strategy document, 1977), quoted in Green, *Thatcher*, p. 115.

43. Turner, *Crisis?*, p. 267.

44. January 31, 1979, The Jimmy Young Programme, BBC Radio 2; quoted in Campbell, *Thatcher, Vol. 1*, p. 423.

45. House of Commons, March 28, 1979 (Vol. 965, cols. 461–470).

46. Quoted in Campbell, *Thatcher, Vol. 1*, p. 427.

47. John Cole, *As It Seemed to Me: Political Memoirs* (London: Phoenix, 1995), p. 187. Emphasis in original.

48. *Leicester Mercury*, April 19, 1979; quoted in Campbell, *Thatcher, Vol. 1*, p. 429.

49. James Prior, *A Balance of Power* (London: Hamish Hamilton, 1986), p. 113.

CHAPTER 5

1. BBC interview, April 27, 1979; quoted in John Campbell, *Margaret Thatcher, Vol. 2: The Iron Lady* (London: Pimlico, 2004), p. 3.

2. Speech in Seoul, Korea; September 3, 1992; Margaret Thatcher Foundation: http://www.margaretthatcher.org/document/108302 (accessed December 18, 2012).

3. Margaret Thatcher, *The Path to Power* (London: HarperCollins, 1996), p. 430.

4. Simon Jenkins, *Thatcher and Sons: A Revolution in Three Acts* (London: Allen Lane, 2006), p. 56.

5. Ibid., p. 56.

6. Alan Clark, *Alan Clark: A Life in His Own Words. The Edited Diaries 1972–1999* (London: Phoenix, 2010), p. 82. Emphasis in original.

7. *Sunday Times*, May, 3, 1981; quoted in Campbell, *Thatcher, Vol. 2*, p. 5.

8. Quoted in Jenkins, *Thatcher and Sons*, p. 78.

9. Peter Clarke, "The Rise and Fall of Thatcherism," *Historical Research*, 72, no. 179 (October 1999): 301–322, p. 314.

10. Speech to Conservative Party Conference, October 10, 1980; Margaret Thatcher Foundation: http://www.margaretthatcher.org/document/104431 (accessed October 4, 2012).

11. House of Commons, July 16, 1981 (Vol. 8, col. 1383).

12. Speech to Finchley Conservative Women, October 22, 1982; Margaret Thatcher Foundation: http://www.margaretthatcher.org/document/105040 (accessed December 18, 2012).

13. Airey Neave Memorial Lecture, March 3, 1980; Margaret Thatcher Foundation: http://www.margaretthatcher.org/document/104318 (accessed January 8, 2013).

14. To Patrick Jenkin; quoted in Nicholas Timmins, *The Five Giants: A Biography of the Welfare State* (London: HarperCollins, 2001), p. 371.

15. Quoted in Campbell, *Thatcher, Vol. 2*, p. 171.

16. Alan Travis, "Margaret Thatcher's Role in Plan to Dismantle Welfare State Revealed," *The Guardian* (London), December 27, 2012.

17. Speech to the Conservative Party Conference, October 8, 1982; Margaret Thatcher Foundation: http://www.margaretthatcher.org/document/105032 (accessed December 18, 2012).

18. Jenkins, *Thatcher and Sons*, p. 87.

19. Nicholas Ridley, *My Style of Government: The Thatcher Years* (London: Hutchinson, 1991), pp. 86–87.

20. Quoted in Andy McSmith, *No Such Thing as Society: A History of Britain in the 1970s* (London: Constable, 2010), p. 80.

21. Quoted in Kathleen Paul, *Whitewashing Britain: Race and Citizenship in the Postwar Era* (Ithaca: Cornell University Press 1997), p. 183.

22. Margaret Thatcher, Press conference after Anglo-Irish Summit, December 8, 1980; Margaret Thatcher Foundation: http://www.margaretthatcher.org/document/104456 (accessed January 8, 2013).

23. Margaret Thatcher, *The Downing Street Years* (London: Harper-Collins, 1995), pp. 68–69.

24. Ibid., p. 157.

25. Ibid., p. 158.

26. Richard Perle, interviewed for *The Thatcher Factor*; quoted in Campbell, *Thatcher, Vol. 2*, p. 267.

27. Thatcher first used this much-repeated phrase in a press conference with West German Chancellor Helmut Kohl in London in February 1983.
28. Quoted in Jenkins, *Thatcher and Sons*, p. 66.
29. Quoted in Paul, *Whitewashing Britain*, p. 185.
30. Campbell, *Thatcher, Vol. 2*, p. 158.
31. Speech to Conservative Rally in Cheltenham, July 3, 1982; Margaret Thatcher Foundation: http://www.margaretthatcher.org/document/104989 (accessed January 8, 2013).

CHAPTER 6

1. Speech to the Conservative Party Conference, October 12, 1984; Margaret Thatcher Foundation: http://www.margaretthatcher.org/document/105763 (accessed December 18, 2012).
2. Remarks on becoming a grandmother, March 3, 1989; Margaret Thatcher Foundation: http://www.margaretthatcher.org/document/107590 (accessed May 15, 2015).
3. Quoted in Henry Ashby Turner, *Germany from Partition to Reunification* (New Haven: Yale University Press, 1992), p. 178.
4. Speech to the Conservative Party Conference, October 10, 1986; Margaret Thatcher Foundation: http://www.margaretthatcher.org/document/106498 (accessed December 18, 2012).
5. Speech to the Conservative Women's Conference, May 13, 1988; quoted in John Campbell, *Margaret Thatcher, Vol. 2: The Iron Lady* (London: Pimlico, 2004), p. 625.
6. Margaret Thatcher, *The Downing Street Years* (London: HarperCollins, 1993), p. 452.
7. Quoted in Campbell, *Thatcher, Vol. 2*, p. 286.
8. Ibid., p. 266.
9. Quoted in Dominic Sandbrook, *State of Emergency: The Way We Were, Britain 1970–1974* (London: Penguin, 2011), p. 151.
10. Margaret Thatcher, *Statecraft: Strategies for a Changing World* (London: Harperx, 2003), p. 320.
11. Quoted in Campbell, *Thatcher, Vol. 2*, p. 65.
12. E. H. H. Green, *Thatcher* (London: Bloomsbury Academic, 2006), p. 177.
13. Thatcher in a BBC interview, 1975; quoted in Green, *Thatcher*, p. 173.
14. BBC interview, *The Poisoned Chalice*, 1996; quoted in Campbell, *Thatcher, Vol. 2*, p. 311.
15. Quoted in Earl A. Reitan, *The Thatcher Revolution: Margaret Thatcher, John Major, Tony Blair and the Transformation of Modern Britain, 1979–2001* (Lanham, MD: Rowman and Littlefield, 2003), p. 101.
16. Quoted in T. W. Heyck and Meredith Veldman, *The Peoples of the British Isles. Volume III: From 1870 to the Present* (Chicago: Lyceum, 2014), p. 345.

17. Green, *Thatcher*, p. 99; Simon Jenkins, *Thatcher and Sons: A Revolution in Three Acts* (London: Allen Lane, 2006) , p. 92.
18. The *Times* (London), November 9, 1985.
19. Quoted in Campbell, *Thatcher, Vol. 2*, p. 360.
20. Ibid., p. 50.
21. Geoffrey Howe, *Conflict of Loyalty* (London Pan Books, 2007), p. 142.
22. Reitan, *The Thatcher Revolution*, p. 162.
23. Campbell, *Thatcher, Vol. 2*, p. 229.
24. Reitan, *The Thatcher Revolution*, p. 78.
25. Quoted in. Campbell, *Thatcher, Vol. 2*, p. 222.
26. Speech to the Institute of Socio-Economic Studies, New York, September 15, 1975; Margaret Thatcher Foundation: http://www.margaretthatcher.org/document/102769 (accessed December 18, 2012).
27. Campbell, *Thatcher, Vol. 2*, p. 247.
28. Reitan, *The Thatcher Revolution*, p. 151.
29. Speech to the Conservative Central Council, Felixstowe, March 15, 1986; Margaret Thatcher Foundation: http://www.margaretthatcher.org/document/106348 (accessed December 18, 2012).
30. Quoted in Reitan, *The Thatcher Revolution*, p. 109.
31. *Faith in the City—A Call for Action by Church and Nation: Report of the Archbishop of Canterbury's Commission on Urban Priority Areas* (xx: xxx, 1985), p. 359. http://www.churchofengland.org/media/55076/faithinthecity.pdf (accessed November 5, 2012).
32. Reitan, *The Thatcher Revolution*, p. 99.

CHAPTER 7

1. Press conference in Paris, November 19, 1990; quoted in John Campbell, *Margaret Thatcher, Vol. 2, The Iron Lady* (London: Pimlico, 2004), p. 730.
2. Ibid., p. 628.
3. Speech to the Conservative Party Conference, October 13, 1989; Margaret Thatcher Foundation: http://www.margaretthatcher.org/document/107789 (accessed December 18, 2012).
4. Campbell, *Thatcher, Vol. 2*, p. 628.
5. Quoted in George Urban, *Diplomacy and Disillusion at the Court of Margaret Thatcher: An Insider's View* (London: I.B. Tauris, 1996), p. 104.
6. Speech at Aspen Institute, Colorado, August 5, 1990; Margaret Thatcher Foundation: http://www.margaretthatcher.org/document/108174 (accessed December 18, 2012).
7. George H. W. Bush and Brent Scowcroft, *A World Transformed* (New York: Doubleday, 1998), p. 352.
8. Television interview, ITN, June 12, 1987; Margaret Thatcher Foundation: http://www.margaretthatcher.org/document/106892 (accessed January 8, 2013).

9. Speech to the Conservative Party Conference, October 9, 1987; Margaret Thatcher Foundation: http://www.margaretthatcher.org/document/106941 (accessed December 18, 2012).

10. Earl A. Reitan, *The Thatcher Revolution: Margaret Thatcher, John Major, Tony Blair and the Transformation of Modern Britain, 1979–2001* (Lanham, MD: Rowman and Littlefield , 2003), p. 136.

11. E. H. H. Green, *Thatcher* (London: Bloomsbury Academic, 2006), p. 84; Simon Jenkins, *Thatcher and Sons: A Revolution in Three Acts* (London: Allen Lane, 2006), p. 105.

12. "Working for Patients," Department of Health and Social Security, 1989; quoted in Jenkins, *Thatcher and Sons*, p. 114.

13. Quoted in Reitan, *The Thatcher Revolution*, p. 102; Campbell, *Thatcher, Vol. 2*, p. 553.

14. Simon Jenkins, *Accountable to None: The Tory Privatisation of Britain* (London: Hamish Hamilton, 1995), p.77.

15. Quoted in Campbell, *Thatcher, Vol. 2*, p. 548.

16. Jenkins, *Accountable to None*, p. 156.

17. Reitan, *The Thatcher Revolution*, p. 66.

18. House of Commons, July 21, 1987 (Vol. 120, col. 204).

19. Campbell, *Thatcher, Vol. 2*, p. 556.

20. Margaret Thatcher, *The Downing Street Years* (London: Pimlico, 1993), p. 661.

21. Chris Patten on *Desert Island Discs*, BBC Radio 4, November 4, 1996; quoted in Campbell, *Thatcher, Vol. 2*, p. 561.

22. Green, *Thatcher*, p. 142.

23. Reitan, *The Thatcher Revolution*, p. 84.

24. Quoted in Hugo Young, *This Blessed Plot: Britain and Europe from Churchill to Blair* (New York: Overlook Press, 1998), p. 345.

25. Speech to the College of Europe, Bruges, September 29, 1988; Margaret Thatcher Foundation: http://www.margaretthatcher.org/document/107332 (accessed December 18, 2012).

26. Speech to the Conservative Party Conference, October 14, 1988; Margaret Thatcher Foundation: http://www.margaretthatcher.org/document/107352 (accessed December 18, 2012).

27. Quoted in Green, *Thatcher*, p. 181.

28. Speech to the Conservative Party Conference, October 14, 1988; Margaret Thatcher Foundation: http://www.margaretthatcher.org/document/107352 (accessed December 16, 2012).

29. Quoted in Reitan, *The Thatcher Revolution*, p. 86.

30. *The Jimmy Young Programme*, July 27, 1988, BBC Radio-2; quoted in Campbell, *Thatcher, Vol. 2*, p. 603.

31. Campbell, *Thatcher, Vol. 2*, p. 719.

32. Geoffrey Howe, *Conflict of Loyalty* (London: Pan Books, 2007), pp. 697–703.

33. Alan Clark, *Alan Clark: A Life in His Own Words. The Edited Diaries 1972–1999* (London: Phoenix, 2010), p. 461, p. 465.

34. *Six O'Clock News*, BBC; "Thatcher Resigns. Six O'Clock News, 221190," http://www.youtube.com/watch?v=Abj8nojrdGY (accessed January 12, 2013).
35. Quoted in Judy Anderson, "Thatcher's resignation stuns Britain," *Baltimore Sun*, November 23, 1990; http://articles.baltimoresun.com/1990-11-23/news/1990327021_1_cabinet-ministers-prime-minister-thatcher (accessed May 22, 2015).

CHAPTER 8

1. Quoted in Peter Clarke, "The Rise and Fall of Thatcherism," *Historical Research*, 72, no. 179 (October 1999): 301–322; p. 303.
2. Earl A. Reitan, *The Thatcher Revolution: Margaret Thatcher, John Major, Tony Blair and the Transformation of Modern Britain, 1979–2001* (Lanham, MD: Rowman and Littlefield, 2003), p. 161.
3. John Rentoul, *Tony Blair, Prime Minister* (London: Faber and Faber 2001), p. 197.
4. Jon Sopel, *Tony Blair, The Moderniser* (New York: Bantam, 1995), p. 208.
5. *The Times* (London), June 10, 2002; quoted in E. H. H. Green, *Thatcher* (London: Bloomsbury Academic, 2006), p. 189.
6. Simon Jenkins, *Thatcher and Sons: A Revolution in Three Acts* (London: Allen Lanex, 2006), p. 194.
7. Speech in The Hague, May 15, 1992; Margaret Thatcher Foundation: http://www.margaretthatcher.org/document/108296 (accessed January 8, 2013).
8. Quoted in Reitan, *The Thatcher Revolution*. p. 143.
9. Ibid., p. 76.
10. Michael H. Hunt, *The World Transformed: 1945 to the Present* (New York: Bedford St. Martin's, 2004), p. 372.
11. Jenkins, *Thatcher and Sons*, p. 152.
12. Daniel Yergin and Joseph Stanislaw, *The Commanding Heights: The Battle Between Government and the Marketplace That Is Remaking the Modern World* (New York: Free Press, 2002), p. 332.
13. Ibid., p. 328; p. xiii.
14. See the poll results in *The Guardian* (London), July 3, 2012.
15. CNN. "Crowds Throng London in March against UK Austerity," October 20, 2012; http://www.cnn.com/2012/10/20/world/europe/uk-anti-austerity-march/index.html (accessed January 12, 2013).
16. See, for example, "Voters Believe Britain Should Leave EU If It Cannot Reclaim Powers, Poll Reveals," *Observer* (London), January 12, 2013; http://www.guardian.co.uk/politics/2013/jan/12/britain-leave-eu-power-poll (accessed January 13, 2013).

17. Quoted in Caroline Davies and Rajeev Syal, "Margaret Thatcher Death: David Cameron Leads Tributes to Iron Lady," *The Guardian*, April 8, 2013; http://www.guardian.co.uk/politics/2013/apr/08/margaret-thatcher-david-cameron-tributes (accessed April 23, 2013).

18. Lauren Turner, "Anti-Thatcher Song 'Ding Dong the Witch Is Dead' Misses Top Spot in Radio 1 Charts," *The Independent*, April 14, 2013; http://www.guardian.co.uk/music/2013/apr/09/anti-thatcher-sentiment-singles-charts (accessed April 11, 2013). The song "Ding, Dong, the Witch Is Dead" comes from the musical *The Wizard of Oz* (1939).

CREDITS

INDEX